PENGUIN BUSINESS
THE NURTURING QUOTIENT

Rajesh Ramakrishnan has worked in the corporate world for the last thirty years across organizations, such as Reckitt, Marico, PepsiCo, *Hindustan Times* and Perfetti. His last role was that of managing director for Perfetti Van Melle India from 2018 to 2023. He was awarded the *Economic Times* Inspiring CEO Award in 2022 and the *ET Ascent* CEO of the Year Award in 2023. Rajesh is a certified executive coach, focusing on CXO–CEO coaching and mentoring, advisory consultant and leadership development facilitator. He is also an award-winning photographer who has had many exhibitions. Rajesh has been on treks to Mount Kilimanjaro, Everest base camp, and Annapurna Base Camp. He is a regular yoga practitioner, an avid foodie and a traveller.

Nirupama Subramanian is a prominent executive coach and leadership development expert with over twenty-five years of experience in this field. She has earlier worked with Citibank, AchieveGlobal and Genpact. She is the founder and CEO of Powerfulife Solutions. She has worked with more than 25,000 leaders across sixty-plus organizations to help them live their potential. Nirupama is the author of two bestselling novels, and her 2021 non-fiction book, *Powerful: The Indian Woman's Guide to Unlocking Her Full Potential,* has become a go-to guide for women leaders. Nirupama is also a TEDx speaker and a board member. She loves yoga, travelling, reading all kinds of books and going for long walks amid nature.

Rajesh and Nirupama have collaborated on various projects over the years—from when they were classmates at XLRI Jamshedpur to bringing up their daughter Kaavya. Together, they also run the family non-profit My Daughter Is Precious, which provides graduate-level scholarships and mentorship for girls from underserved families. *The Nurturing Quotient* is their first book together.

ADVANCE PRAISE FOR THE BOOK

'After permissions, capital and technology became available to all, people and culture have become the only real differentiators for a business. We need to dream, and we need people to give shape to our thoughts. Rajesh and Nirupama's *The Nurturing Quotient* explains the "why and how to" of this process'—**Harit Nagpal, MD and CEO, Tata Play Ltd**

'Acting on nurturing leadership skills tends to come in too low a dose or a bit late to the game for many of us in the midst of driving high performance in times of equally high levels of change. Let it be a wake-up call for all of us that ultimately, enduring performance requires mastering nurturing leadership for the ones we work with and even ourselves. Nirupama and Rajesh have explored this important aspect of leadership in their book and brought it alive through the experiences of more than a hundred leaders across different industries'—**Mieke Van de Capelle, chief human resources officer, DSM-Firmenich**

'In today's dynamic and unpredictable world, leadership demands more than just strategy and execution; it requires depth, humanity and a commitment to growth. *The Nurturing Quotient* beautifully captures these essential qualities, providing a compelling blueprint for leaders to thrive both professionally and personally. By weaving together rich insights, actionable frameworks and the lived experiences of leaders from diverse industries, Rajesh Ramakrishnan and Nirupama Subramanian have created a guide that is both practical and profound. As someone who has had the privilege of contributing to this work, I am inspired by its emphasis on qualities such as humility, empathy and openness, which are crucial for building strong teams and resilient organizations. This approach is not just relevant but imperative in shaping leaders who can balance ambition with compassion and lead with authenticity and impact. *The Nurturing Quotient* is a must-read for leaders aiming to create meaningful change in today's complex world'—**Ashish Dhawan, founder and chairman, The Convergence Foundation**

'Rajesh and Nirupama have written a book that is a compelling read on leading with care, compassion and empathy. The lived experiences of nurturing self and others of over a hundred leaders studied in the book leave the readers with many practical, non-preachy, ready-to-start ways of creating authentic paths of personal and professional growth guided by a strong sense of purpose'—**Pramath Raj Sinha, founder and trustee, Ashoka University**

'While people are obsessing about AI, nurturing leadership is a topic that no algorithm can ever teach you. Based on their personal experience and the lived experiences of over a hundred CEOs, Rajesh and Nirupama have beautifully captured how leaders not just lead, they actually nurture and grow themselves and others'—**Pavan Bhatia, founder, GenWE**

'*The Nurturing Quotient* is a valuable contribution from Rajesh and Nirupama on how to link leadership, self and others to the vital theme of "nurturing". This alone lends "character" to the leadership journey and process, and using leadership journeys, they beautifully illustrate this vital link. A must-read for all leaders—young and not-so-young—on how to infuse the magic touch of nurturing in a systematic manner to be more effective leaders and to keep their teams inspired'—**Suresh Narayanan, chairman and managing director, Nestlé India**

'We have all experienced leaders who only cared about performance and were difficult. And others who inspired us, developed us and helped us grow. Who would you rather work with? *The Nurturing Quotient* by Rajesh and Nirupama captures the essence of this important shift in leadership style.

It highlights the criticality of nurturing oneself so that one can fully nurture others through HOPE (humility, openness, patience and empathy)'—**Anand Kripalu, managing director and global CEO, EPL Ltd**

'In a rapidly changing world, effective leadership goes beyond traditional authority; it requires a nurturing touch that fosters growth and collaboration. In *The Nurturing Quotient*, Rajesh and Nirupama introduce the transformative HOPE framework—an innovative approach rooted in humility, openness, patience and empathy. This insightful guide delves into the essential qualities that every leader should embody to inspire and empower their teams. Through practical strategies such as mentoring, coaching, inspiring, listening and empowering, the authors illuminate how nurturing leaders create an environment where individuals thrive and organizations flourish. Drawing on real-world examples and actionable advice, *The Nurturing Quotient* is a compelling read for anyone aspiring to lead with purpose and compassion. Discover how to cultivate a leadership style that not only achieves results but also makes a lasting impact on the lives of those you lead. Embrace the journey of nurturing leadership and unlock the potential within yourself and your team'—**Sanjiv Mehta, former chair/CEO, Hindustan Lever, and executive chairman, L Catterton India**

'*The Nurturing Quotient* serves as a practical guide for leaders who seek to leave a lasting impact by building resilient teams and purpose-driven organizations. As I was sharing my thoughts with Rajesh and Nirupama, I was reminded of my own experiences of how leaders/mentors I have looked up to have nurtured my curiosity and shaped me into who I am today. Leaders ought to nurture the next generation by balancing purpose with performance, countering challenges with compassion and empowering through empathy. Through this book, Rajesh and Nirupama have captured this balance beautifully, offering insights and examples that will resonate with leaders at every stage of their careers and enable them to build a legacy, for themselves and those whose lives they touch. Enjoy reading the book and do assess your own Nurturing Quotient'—**Hemant Malik, executive director, ITC Ltd**

'Rajesh and Nirupama provide useful and interesting insights for leaders on the theme of nurturing self and others. Being a leader requires us to demonstrate certain nurturing qualities of humility, openness, patience and empathy (HOPE) so that we can bring our best selves to work and develop others to become successful leaders. I relate to many of these practices to mentor, inspire and empower teams I have worked with. This book not only provides insights but also best practices that are easy to implement for anyone who aspires to grow and help others grow'—**Amit Jain, chairman, Sanofi CHC and Collective Newsroom (BBC News)**

'*The Nurturing Quotient* is a timely and very useful read. Both Rajesh and Nirupama have used their own experiences and the experiences and insights of leaders to bring this book to life'—**Sucheta Govil, chief commercial officer, Covestro**

'Today's BANI (Brittle, Anxious, Non-linear and Incomprehensible) world requires conscientious and caring leaders who have mastery over both their inner and outer game. Rajesh and Nirupama have poured out their years of corporate experience to build the nurturing leadership model. *The Nurturing Quotient* is not just a concept that warms your heart; it is also a playbook that offers an implementation-worthy toolkit to every leader and individual yearning to make a real difference. A must-read, easy-to-follow guide for every individual'—**Kedar Lele, managing director, Castrol India Ltd**

'An inspiring read! Nirupama and Rajesh have shone the light on the ability of leaders to nurture and grow colleagues.

In my belief, this is what distinguishes great leaders from good ones and is a "must-have quality" for aspiring inspirational leaders'—**Bharat Puri, managing director, Pidilite Industries**

'Rajesh and Nirupama have done a great job of capturing the essence of what it takes to be a truly impactful leader. Leadership is not just about achieving results; it is a demanding journey that requires intentional effort to manage one's own energy while fostering the growth of others. This book offers valuable insights and practical strategies that make leadership development both accessible and actionable'—**Debjani Ghosh, former president, NASSCOM**

'Today's CEOs need to manage often conflicting demands and continue to grow the business and people while staying relevant and energized. Rajesh and Nirupama introduce the concept of the Nurturing Quotient, which is about nurturing the self and nurturing others. Through the lived examples of over a hundred leaders whom they have spoken to, they share simple and practical ways in which aspiring leaders can become nurturing leaders'—**Harsh Mariwala, chairman, Marico Limited**

'A CEO's job is a privilege, a platform to make a dent in the universe. That said, it is also demanding, lonely and relentless. This idea that you can go all in on your career and later reconcile with other aspects of your life is seductive but not true. Time has to matter *now*, not just in the pursuit of more. Rajesh and Nirupama have pulled together incredible insights on nurturing yourself and others around you by taking care of your body, mind and soul. This is the book for every leader, and I can't recommend this enough'—**Puneet Chandok, president, Microsoft (India and South Asia)**

'Reading *The Nurturing Quotient* felt like sitting down with two wise friends who have walked the path, stumbled, learnt and now gently offer what they have gathered. Rajesh and

Nirupama write with honesty and heart, weaving stories that stay with you long after you have flipped the last page. What struck me most was how they reframe leadership—not as performance but as presence, not as control but as care. In a time of noise and burnout, this book offers a quiet, radical shift: that nurturing isn't soft—it's strategic, sustaining and urgently needed. A compelling guide for anyone ready to lead with more wholeness'—**Vivek Gambhir, venture partner and operating adviser**

'As an adviser to organizations on managing talent in the AI economy, I believe succession planning must go beyond performance and potential to include the ability to nurture. Manager training still has MILEs to go—Mentor, Inspire, Listen, Empower—and this book shows the way. It offers a new vocabulary and everyday practices for human-centred growth. *The Nurturing Quotient* reframes leadership by spotlighting mental, emotional and spiritual energy as core to sustainable impact. The framework is intuitive and easy to integrate into the business'—**Abhijit Bhaduri, former partner and global head, L&D, Microsoft**

THE NURTURING QUOTIENT

How to Grow Yourself and Others
for Leadership Success

**RAJESH RAMAKRISHNAN
NIRUPAMA SUBRAMANIAN**

PENGUIN
BUSINESS

An imprint of Penguin Random House

PENGUIN BUSINESS

Penguin Business is an imprint of the Penguin Random House group of companies whose addresses can be found at global.penguinrandomhouse.com

Published by Penguin Random House India Pvt. Ltd
4th Floor, Capital Tower 1, MG Road,
Gurugram 122 002, Haryana, India

First published in Penguin Business by Penguin Random House India 2025

Copyright © Rajesh Ramakrishnan and Nirupama Subramanian 2025

All rights reserved

10 9 8 7 6 5 4 3 2 1

The views and opinions expressed in this book are the authors' own and the facts are as reported by them which have been verified to the extent possible, and the publishers are not in any way liable for the same.

Please note that no part of this book may be used or reproduced in any manner for the purpose of training artificial intelligence technologies or systems.

ISBN 9780143474876

Typeset in Sabon LT Pro by MAP Systems, Bengaluru, India

This book is sold subject to the condition that it shall not, by way of trade or otherwise, be lent, resold, hired out or otherwise circulated without the publisher's prior consent in any form of binding or cover other than that in which it is published and without a similar condition including this condition being imposed on the subsequent purchaser.

www.penguin.co.in

Scan QR code to access the Penguin Random House India website

Contents

Foreword   xiii
Preface   xv

Section I: The Why of Nurturing Leadership

1. The Challenges That Leaders Face   3
2. The Importance of Nurturing Leadership   27

Section II: Growing the Self

3. Nurture the Self   39
4. Nourish Your Body   45
5. Sharpen Your Mind   63
6. Open Your Heart   82
7. Enrich Your Soul   96

Section III: Growing Others

8. Nurture Others   115
9. Mentor and Coach Others   129
10. Inspire to Grow   143
11. Listen Actively   162
12. Empower to Thrive   177

Section IV: Nurturing as a Practice

13. Who We Are Is How We Nurture   197
14. Strike the Right Balance   213
15. Bringing It All Together   227

Acknowledgements   235
Notes   243

Foreword

A leader is but an ordinary man doing extraordinary things. Rajesh and Nirupama deftly navigate the journey of an ordinary person and the circumstances that shape them to do extraordinary things in this book aptly titled *The Nurturing Quotient*. In today's world, while IQ and EQ are important, the concept of NQ is becoming increasingly relevant. This book focuses on nurturing oneself along the four dimensions of physical, mental, emotional and spiritual well-being, and nurturing others through the four behaviours of MILE: mentoring, inspiring, listening and empowering.

At first glance, this book appears to be a compilation of experiences from industry leaders, but co-authors Rajesh and Nirupama make it much more than that. A corporate leader himself, with over thirty years of experience in the industry, Rajesh brings in the subtle nuances that bring out the aspects of leadership every aspiring leader needs to understand. On the other hand, being a leadership coach and facilitator for over two decades, Nirupama adds her special touch to help people make sense of the insights and best practices shared in the book.

I have had the good fortune to know several leaders featured in the book, some during my leadership journey at Hindustan Unilever. There are those who have witnessed my 'glorious failures' that helped me learn the lessons of leadership; and those who have been a part of my successes.

This book features several examples of such challenges and the successes that come out of it. What's interesting is the way the authors succinctly put together the learnings from these challenges. In this book, you will find what it takes to balance work and personal life as you embark upon the leadership journey. In this book, you will learn how to make every failure a stepping stone to success. In this book, you will come face to face with real-life challenges that leaders face—of managing personal relationships, of well-being, of navigating the paradigm shift that we are all seeing in work culture.

This is a book that can be your guide—through times when the leadership journey seems daunting, and there are no clear answers. I have always believed that leaders build leaders, and by narrating leadership stories that provide solutions, Rajesh and Nirupama have created what can only be described as a playbook for aspiring leaders in these fast-changing times.

25 April 2025

Nitin Paranjpe
chairman, Hindustan Unilever Ltd

Preface

How We Came to Write This Book

'If there's a book that you want to read, but it hasn't been written yet, then you must write it.'

—Toni Anderson

It all started sometime in early 2023, when we (Rajesh and Nirupama) were having a dinner table discussion. Rajesh, who was the managing director of Perfetti Van Melle India, and Nirupama, a leadership coach and facilitator, were discussing their day. Nirupama had completed a leadership development workshop, and Rajesh had finished a long meeting with the management committee.

One of the leaders in Nirupama's workshop had remarked, 'It shouldn't have to be so stressful to be a leader. I feel that I have to do a hundred things every day and be a hundred different things to a hundred different people.'

Rajesh was discussing some tough people-related decisions that needed to be made at work. He was talking about the ongoing struggle to balance his natural empathetic, caring nature with a harsher pragmatic business reality.

We then changed the subject to other things—our yoga teacher had given us some work for the class the next morning. We were starting a new cohort of students for the non-profit that we run together as a family—My Daughter Is Precious—where we provide scholarships and mentorships for girls from underserved families to complete their higher education. Rajesh was working on a photography project around the theme of exploring the number 7 from multiple perspectives. Nirupama mentioned that people were asking about her next book. We both were excited about our daughter's graduation from University of Southern California, Los Angeles, that summer. We love travelling, so we were combining the trip for her graduation with a holiday to a new place.

Rajesh had successfully delivered a talk on 'Leadership Lessons from Photography', where he drew connections between being a photographer and a leader. The talk had elicited a great response from the group of leaders.

Nirupama had integrated the concepts from her last book, *Powerful: The Indian Woman's Guide to Unlocking Her Full Potential*,[1] into her work on diversity and inclusion and gender. What started as an idea around feminine powers had become the 'Powerfulife' system.

We realized that all these things are connected. Our life practices impacted our work, and the work flowed into our lives. The fact that we had a wide range of interests outside work helped us do our work better, with less stress and more joy. While everyone spoke about work–life balance, we felt that it was more about energy balance.

We had heard a lot about the blurring of work–life boundaries after the Covid-19 pandemic. The concept of switching off from work is impossible today. There is no clear demarcation between office space and home space; office time and personal time, work colleagues and personal friends are often the same.

What were the leaders, the CEOs and the MDs who were in charge of the organizations doing about it? Is a different model of leadership required for these times?

Many articles were published about leading through the crisis of the pandemic and the qualities that were required to steer organizations through troubled times. A McKinsey study[2] stated that the four qualities of awareness, empathy, vulnerability and compassion are the traits needed to tide over the crisis and move towards recovery. Words such as mental and physical health, employee well-being and 'workcations' were being used along with profits, growth and market share.

Yet, most of the leaders in positions of power today are Baby Boomers (people born between 1946 and 1964) and Gen X (people born between 1965 and 1980). We grew up in an era where long hours were a given and the neglect of personal well-being in favour of loyalty to the collective was a noble ideal. Vacations were a perk, and personal time off or mental health days were not a part of the organizational lexicon. There was a joke in the multinational bank where Nirupama first worked that ulcers were a badge of high achievement!

Command and control was the preferred leadership style. A senior leader at a large public sector bank mentioned during a coaching session with Nirupama that he had always believed that listening to others was a sign of weakness. He felt that as a leader, he had to show strength through unilateral decision-making. In our cultural context, honouring the hierarchy was a sign of respect. A leader could not afford to be vulnerable or show signs of humility due to the fear that it could be interpreted as incompetence or weakness.

There are plenty of leadership theories, models, frameworks and concepts. Books on leadership are being written every month. None of the theories are wrong. A leader's work is not easy. As one goes higher up the ladder, the risks and trade-offs increase. The nature of the job becomes more complicated and demanding. In a rapidly changing world, where even the term used to describe it—VUCA (volatile, uncertain, complex and ambiguous)—morphs into BANI (brittle, anxious, non-linear and incomprehensible), leadership too must be going through its own evolution. Interestingly, the acronym BANI was coined in 2020 by American anthropologist, futurist and author Jamais Cascio in an article titled 'Age of Chaos'[3]. He felt that VUCA no longer described the new world order. Unlike VUCA, BANI also speaks to the primary emotion that this rapidly changing world triggers—anxiety. This heightened anxiety stems from stress, information overload and lack of control over an unpredictable world.

What does a leader's role look like in this evolving, uncertain world?

What *should* it look like?

As skills, tools, technology and the environment undergo rapid changes and become more complex, it is more important for leaders to learn and evolve. The CEO has not yet been replaced by a machine. The CEO remains human with all the beauty, complexity and unpredictability associated with the species. As a species, we have transitioned from the credo of 'survival of the fittest' to 'survival of the smartest'. However, in this new age of rapid technological changes and artificial intelligence, merely being physically strong and technically smart is no longer enough.

We believe that everyone who aspires to a position of high responsibility and creates impact at scale and sustainable growth needs to practise 'Nurturing Leadership'.

Intelligence quotient (IQ), emotional quotient (EQ) and even spiritual quotient (SQ) have all been used as measures of leadership success. We have heard of the saying: IQ gets you hired but EQ gets you promoted. We believe that nurturing quotient (NQ) is necessary to keep that promotion—especially as the role gets more demanding and challenging.

We define NQ as the ability to consistently nurture self and others for personal and professional growth. NQ is a measure of Nurturing Leadership.

How we approached the book:

1. We examined our lived experiences over the last fifty-plus years as individuals and as leaders. Even though we were aligned in many values, there were differences in our preferences and styles of nurturing ourselves and others.
2. We read many other books and articles on the themes and examined relevant research and best practices
3. We also wanted this book to be real and not just theory. We interviewed 117 leaders—CEOs of established organizations, founders and entrepreneurs, leaders from the armed forces, government and heads of nonprofits. We asked these leaders a few questions.
    - What are some challenges you face as a leader, and how does this impact you personally?
    - What are the ways in which you nurture yourself?
    - What are the ways in which you nurture others?
    - We have used the inputs from this primary research and also from some other secondary sources of data to answer the WHY of Nurturing Leadership. We have identified the commonly

used best practices and practical, everyday ways to nurture the self and others from these lived experiences of leaders. This answers the WHAT and HOW of Nurturing Leadership. When we examined the answers to these questions, we could also identify the factors that determined HOW COME or the reasons behind the WHAT. We saw interesting variations and different pulls along the polarities that leaders needed to balance to nurture self and others.

Together, these give a deep and comprehensive view of Nurturing Leadership. Through this book, we wish to provide a new way of not just leading organizations but also leading a more holistic, well-balanced and joyful life. You do not have to be a leader at scale or a CEO to use these concepts. If a busy CEO with multiple responsibilities can prioritize self-care and care for others, we can all learn from them and do the same at any stage of life.

Section I

The Why of Nurturing Leadership

1

The Challenges That Leaders Face

'Hard times don't create heroes. It is during the hard times when the "hero" within us is revealed.'

—Bob Riley

'Where am I?' wondered Vipul. After a while, all business class lounges in international airports begin to look the same. For a minute, he wondered if he was travelling from Mumbai to a new destination or returning from . . . where . . . Cairo? or Doha? His brain felt numb, his eyes were smarting and his throat itched with an irritating dryness. He looked at his phone, hoping for a clue. The time was 3.45 a.m.! There was a delectable spread of food at the buffet counter, but Vipul had no appetite. He had put on three kilos in the last month. He had to get to the gym . . . but when?

It was just six months since Vipul was appointed as president for AMEA (Asia, Middle East and Africa) at Eat Well, Inc., one of the world's largest companies in the food industry. From being the India CEO to going on to lead eighteen countries across three geographies was a huge promotion. It was a great gift on his fifty-second birthday. He had been ecstatic at the news; now he was just exhausted. He had not bargained for fifteen days of international travel in a month. His body did not seem to be keeping pace with his career! He also needed to spend more time with his daughter Maya. In a year, she would be in college in another country! He missed those father–daughter bonding times when they went to Churchgate for ice cream sandwiches.

Vipul had welcomed the opportunity to manage people across cultures—it was the next level of leadership for him; that was what he had told Brigitta, the Global CEO. The team in Nigeria was struggling; they needed more of his time, but so did the team in Kenya. Both the teams were so different—he had thought Africa was a homogenous continent, but now he knew he was totally wrong. He wished he had time to mentor his new team but ended up cancelling the past few sessions due to other business commitments.

His phone beeped with a notification from a news website. He barely registered that Israel had launched an offensive strike in Gaza. Now that would affect his operations in the Middle East! He was looking forward to a quiet evening at home after returning, but now he needed to get on a call again to figure out how the Middle Eastern crisis would affect the business.

He was supposed to be the most powerful man in his country at Eat Well, Inc., yet he felt that he had no control over his time. He wanted to be disciplined and make time for other important things, but time was slipping away from him.

* * *

'Mom, I will fail in my board exams,' wailed Aliya. 'I hate math. I don't want to do this anymore. The tuition classes are of no use.'

Nusrat took a deep breath and prepared her 'mom face'. 'Of course, you won't fail. I will help you with math. See, it is not so hard.' She knew that there was a call with her global managers at 9 p.m. That gave her twelve minutes to help Aliya to solve her math problems and become confident and ready for the exam the next day.

Impossible!

'Why don't you take a break and get a snack?' Nusrat suggested, adding, 'I will quickly wrap up this meeting, and then we can spend some more time together.' She constantly felt guilty about not being there for Aliya. Two more years, she thought to herself and felt more guilty about the fact that she was looking forward to Aliya leaving home for college.

She quickly went to her room and prepared her 'work face'—a dash of lipstick and a touch-up with her compact. Nusrat was now the managing director of Boyds India, the largest global capability centre for Boyds Bank, UK. Amelia and Pedro, her two bosses, wanted to discuss the increasing attrition numbers at the centre. There had been a messy POSH case, which had generated some adverse publicity—these Gen Zs had no idea how to behave during the company offsite. She was going to suggest that they stop serving alcohol at these parties. Managing 5000 employees with an average age of twenty-eight was no party. She thought she was a good leader but somehow, she did not know how to inspire and motivate these young employees. Some of them seemed so entitled, others had no sense of purpose and almost all of them wanted flexi hours and work life balance without putting in the hard work that the job required. If they didn't get a promotion within a year, they threatened to quit!

Her phone buzzed with WhatsApp messages. She took a quick look. Her yoga instructor had texted: 'Ma'am, are you cancelling again for tomorrow? You will still have to pay the full fees.' She had just managed three classes during the last month. She needed to do better. But how could she get up any earlier? She was up at 5.30 a.m. to make Aliya's lunch and get the house in order. She barely got fifteen minutes to drink her tea in peace.

Her 'Girls Just Wanna Have Fun' group had a slew of messages asking her for a date for the next trip. She longed to get away with her three best friends from college, they always gave her a huge energy boost but she could not see any opportunity for a break for the next six to eight months. Zaheer's job involved a lot of travel, and it was difficult for her to get away, leaving Aliya alone. If at all she got any free time, she went home to Lucknow to be with her mother for a few days.

Her computer came alive with the faces of her bosses, and Nusrat opened her PowerPoint presentation. She stifled a yawn and hoped she would be awake and alert for the next hour.

* * *

'Did I do the right thing?' Abhay asked his reflection. He had been doing this for the past few days, every time he looked in the mirror. It had not been easy to quit his job as product manager in one of the world's largest organizations, leave a brand that had become a household name, a steady income and the promise of a long, stable career. But he was quite sure that the corporate world was not for him.

It had been three years since he, Mithila and Shashank had left their comfortable jobs to set up GreenTech. It had been so exciting at first, the rush of being your own boss, the thrill of getting the first series of funding, setting up an office, hiring the first employee . . . But now, the pressures were just mounting.

He was dreading the investor meeting tomorrow. The numbers did not look promising. He had left the financials to Shashank and had focused on building the product, getting the right technology. But getting the right people was proving to be a bigger challenge. He and Mithila could not agree on the talent acquisition plan. Now, three senior people had just quit, citing personal reasons. The attrition levels at the junior levels were also higher than the industry standard. Everyone he knew in the startup world worked long and hard. Having fourteen- to sixteen-hour days was common. It had to be this way if you wanted to grow quickly. Why couldn't others have the same level of commitment and ownership as him? Why could others not have his drive and ambition? What was the point of having these weak emotional people who couldn't take a bit of constructive criticism?

During the last meeting, there were questions on his leadership style. 'What are you doing about creating the right culture with the right values?' one of the board members had asked. She had spoken about the importance of having a leadership style that demonstrated empathy and deep listening. How could they question him about his leadership style? At this stage, was it not about getting the job done quickly and efficiently? Did he have to get into this fluffy human resources stuff?

He had only three years to go to fulfil his dream of being featured in the '40 under 40' list of entrepreneurs.

It looked like a fantasy at this stage. He felt that he was heading to a burnout, yet he was unable to get off this treadmill.

'Get a mentor or a coach,' the board member had suggested. Just as Menaka had suggested couples therapy to salvage their marriage. He had been dismissive of both ideas. Coaching and therapy would leave no time for real work!

Now Abhay wondered if he needed help.

* * *

These stories are common. They are based on real situations that we have seen and heard.

The leader faces an ever-changing environment with multiple challenges. Every leader is also a parent, partner, friend and human. As we bring our whole selves into work, the challenges get compounded. In fact, the nature of challenges faced by a leader today is very different from challenges faced by a leader fifty years ago.

Ron Heifetz and Martin Linsky describe two kinds of challenges in their book *Adaptive Leadership*[4]—*Technical Challenges and Adaptive Challenges*.

Technical challenges are:

1. Easy to identify.
2. Often lend themselves to quick and concrete solutions.
3. Often can be solved by an authority or expert.
4. People are generally receptive to technical solutions.
5. Technical solutions can often be implemented quickly—even by decree.

Adaptive challenges, on the other hand, are:

1. Difficult to identify and easy to deny.
2. Solutions are unknown, and previous solutions may not work.
3. Require changes in values, beliefs, roles, relationships and approaches on how to accomplish goals.
4. Require change in numerous places; usually cross organizational boundaries, therefore requires systems thinking.
5. Involves experimentation and smart risks.

The biggest mistake of leadership is applying technical solutions for adaptive challenges. Many people apply solutions that have worked in other situations in the past but fail to take sufficiently into account the complexity of the new problem situation and end up applying technical fixes. The failure to take into account the complexity of the problem and treat it like any other analytical, expert task that can be separated from the cultural and political human dimensions of the situation is a primary cause of low success rates in effective implementation.

In the conversations we had with several leaders in India and abroad, across diverse sectors, one thing was clear—the challenges and demands of a leader today are immense and unprecedented.

We could see four broad categories of challenges.

Macro-environment challenges

Political uncertainty, emerging technologies and supply chain headaches are among the biggest worries facing global CEOs in 2023, according to the latest instalment of an annual study done by KPMG.[5] Today's leaders need to deal with unprecedented challenges across the macro environment.

Geopolitical

The geopolitical situation in one part of the world affects the supply chains of an organization in the other end of the globe. Economic factors such as inflation, fluctuations in the currency rates and elasticities of demand and supply can cause havoc in the planning and managing of annual operating plans.

'When there was war in Ukraine, it affected business across the world. Wheat supply, freight prices, energy requirement for production—all of these were disrupted,' says **Mohit Anand, MD (AMEA) of Kellanova.**

Sucheta Govil, chief commercial officer, Covestro, feels that there is no rule book today. 'The world order led by economic growth is no longer there. Now there is more flux, and business and politics are more intertwined than ever before.'

Deepak Iyer, president of AMEA for Mondelēz, talks about the worry of failed states. He says, 'Some countries in emerging markets have long-term potential. However, in the short term, they are often challenged due to external and internal volatility that impacts growth.'

Regulatory

Regulatory requirements are also changing, especially in India. Listed companies have to deal with reporting requirements and media scrutiny. Profitable growth, while playing by the rules of the game in an era of constant media attention, is a challenge. **Sanjiv Mehta, former chair/CEO, Hindustan Unilever Ltd and chairman, L Catterton India,** believes that 'Leaders need to ensure profitable sustainable growth even as they tackle economic, geopolitical and regulatory challenges.'

Technology

Artificial intelligence (AI) and disruptive technologies can pose both opportunities and challenges for each and every business. A KPMG study reports that in India, 77 per cent of CEOs (and globally, 82 per cent) view generative AI as a double-edged sword, as it can both enhance cybersecurity efforts and create new vulnerabilities for adversaries to exploit.

Hina Nagarajan, MD of Diageo, believes that, 'With the advancement in technologies like data, analytics and AI, it's important to equip the workforce with the skills to stay competitive in the future, drive innovation and meet strategic challenges in the digital age.'

Business challenges

The way we do business is continuously evolving. Even as events unfold across the globe in a chaotic and unforeseen manner, the leader needs to keep the business running at optimum capacity. This involves the usual operational challenges of managing stakeholders, tackling unions, dealing with the local government regulations and, at the same time, ensuring that the business goals are met.

Managing stakeholders

Managing multiple stakeholders and their often conflicting priorities in itself is a huge challenge that leaders face today. Articulating and aligning the larger vision of the organization with these stakeholders and adding value to them is key for success. These challenges are often nuanced and usually do not have that one right answer. **Harsh Mariwala, chairman of Marico Industries,** says, 'All stakeholders are critical and interconnected, and one of the key challenges for leaders today is to add value to a diverse set of stakeholders with multiple and often conflicting needs.'

Changing face of competition

Another key business challenge is competition and how it is getting redefined. Competition in today's world is no longer limited to traditional forms of competition as we understood in the past. **Shiv Shivakumar, operating partner, Advent International,** has an insight into competition: 'Product life cycles are getting shortened by the day. The nature of competition is also changing; today someone who is not at all connected with your industry can be your competition.' **Aditya Ghosh, founder of Homage Ventures and co-founder of Akasa Air,** adds, 'Moats are getting commoditized very quickly, competitive advantages are losing relevance sooner than before and businesses need to have a structural competitive advantage which is difficult to copy.'

Evolving business models

The changes happening in the environment and in consumer behaviour are forcing companies to relook at their business models. **Varun Berry, MD and vice-chairman, Britannia Industries,** stresses the need to 'figure out new business models leveraging the best of both worlds—the old economy companies and startups'.

Apurva Purohit, founder of Aazol, says, 'Businesses are going through big swings over short periods of time.

Running a sustainable business, especially in people-intensive businesses, is a big challenge.'

Creating consumer and customer value profitably in an inflationary environment is another key challenge. **Sussanne Arfelt, former CEO of Royal Greenland,** highlights another leadership dilemma: 'Leaders need to manage inflationary pressures and yet continue to offer consumers value for which they are willing to pay for.'

Sustainability and governance

A new area to be addressed by organizations is ESG (environment, social and governance), even as they strive for profitable and sustainable growth that is people and planet friendly. Shareholder expectations around ESG imply that CEOs now need to see ESG as a core component of strategy and execution. SEBI now mandates that the top 1000 companies by market capitalization in India have to disclose their ESG activities under the BRSR (business responsibility and sustainability reporting) framework. Large organizations need to ensure that their vendors and suppliers are compliant with ESG norms as well. This could impact the supply chain process as well as vendor relationships in a highly competitive market.

Ram Raghavan, global president of oral care, Colgate, mentions the fact that, 'Stakeholder demands have moved from just the what to the how as well. There is now more focus on social impact, giving back to the community, ethics and compliance.'

People challenges

No leader can do everything by themselves. In order to keep the business running at optimum levels, the leader needs to have the right people with the right capability at the right level to effectively manage the business. This involves a deep level of understanding of the different cohorts that make up today's workforce, what they are looking for and how to provide that in a way that meets their goals as well as the organizational goals.

Attracting and retaining talent

All the leaders we spoke to agreed that acquiring, retaining and growing talent was a major challenge. **Ritesh Gauba, country general manager (India) at pladis Global,** talks about a challenge that is typical for smaller organizations and many startups. He says, 'While we are a small organization, in the process of building for the future, helping my team to see the larger vision and getting them to believe in that vision is a key challenge.'

Saugata Gupta, MD and CEO of Marico Limited, also faces a problem in attracting talent. He says, 'Young people don't want to do sales stints anymore; they want to become marketers straight away. The FMCG industry is no longer seen as the only aspirational sector.'

Dr Parag Rindani, CEO of Wockhardt Hospitals, faces a huge human resource shortage in the healthcare sector. Many qualified people want to work overseas. Attrition makes it difficult to foster a sense of dedication and empathy, especially with freshly passed out graduates.

Vineeta Singh, co-founder and CEO of SUGAR Cosmetics, talks about the people-related challenges that startups face. 'Retaining top talent is one of them. The other is that the percolation of the culture within the organization often does not keep pace with the growth of the organization. And the third one is about the constant need to upgrade existing talent in a fast-growing company.'

Deep Kalra, founder and CEO of Makemytrip, says, 'Attracting and retaining top talent in today's competitive environment is also an ongoing challenge. Our ability to not only identify and develop but also inspire and retain talent that can think creatively, execute effectively and lead with purpose is critical to our continued success.'

'How I balance the overall strategy with delivering it through people is a constant challenge,' agrees **Rajiv Rajgopal, chairman and MD, Akzo Nobel India**.

Managing a multigenerational workforce

The composition of the workforce has changed significantly over the past few years. The Gen Z you hired six months ago wants to quit and explore the world. A thirty-five-year-old manager wants to start something on her own. The fifty-year-old team member wants to take a sabbatical to recharge himself.

The changing demographics of the population, the demands of Gen Z and Millennials and a multitude of career options imply that leaders need to find new ways of engaging and leading people. Gone are the days when people joined a company and stayed there until retirement. Leaders need to weave a common culture across generations yet retain the core aspects of diversity in thinking.

Apurva Purohit says, 'Dealing with multiple cohorts of varied age groups brings in several multi-generational challenges. They grew up in different contexts, have different needs and have diverse views on topics such as results, hierarchy, etc. Managing them is a challenge and leaders need to have different styles of leadership for different folks.'

Uday Shankar Sinha, regional MD, Heineken, Asia Pacific, says, 'Getting diverse teams to work together in a collaborative manner towards aligned organizational goals is not easy.'

'For me, the need as a leader is to set a vision and purpose for people and to then provide the leadership that allows our people to give the best they can to meet their personal needs and goals as well as those of the organization. The changing needs of the generations makes this ever more challenging and rewarding,' says **Clive Kornitzer, group COO, OSB Group PLC**.

A Deloitte survey[6] of Millennials and Gen Z across forty-five countries showed some interesting findings. Over the three-year period from 2019–2021, they were becoming disenchanted with the world of business. Close to 70 per cent of Millennials and Gen Z believed that businesses focused on their own agenda and not on society and had no other ambition apart from making money.

The top three concerns of this population were healthcare, climate change and unemployment. Forty-nine per cent of Millennials say that they feel anxious and stressed all the time, and they want their employers to address this issue. People want flexibility, support and care and yet may not be willing to sign their lives away to the corporation. How do leaders motivate these employees to give their best?

Narmeen Khan, managing director Malaysia and Singapore for Mondelēz, thinks that for the new generation, the style of working has changed, expectations have evolved. 'They need more flexibility; they can afford to be choosy. Work has to be aligned to their values and purpose. Leaders need to figure out how to do that,' she says.

Geetika Mehta, MD at Nivea India, says, 'Inspiring today's young workforce, who have a very different world view, and instilling passion in them is a key challenge.'

The talent pool is also becoming increasingly diverse across not just generations but also gender, geography, sexual orientation and abilities. The social aspect of ESG reporting as well as shareholder and brand requirements imply that managers need to be comfortable with diversity in the workplace and ensure that all voices are heard. Building an inclusive culture comes from the top, and CEOs need to be role models for diversity, equity and inclusion (DEI) initiatives and champion new behaviours that are centred on emotional intelligence.

Aligning career drivers

There was a time, a few decades ago, when building a career was seen as one of the key drivers for every young aspiring professional. To join a company at an entry-level, serve time and work one's way up was the norm. Typically, professionals worked in three to five companies over the course of their careers. Today, it's no longer so. There is a shift in the mindset of the professionals who are now exposed to many more ways of engagement with organizations, and they are happily embracing them. Older employees want to 'retire' early and focus on other aspects of their lives. Taking a career break for higher studies or care-giving responsibilities is not uncommon.

Today, employees 'volunteer' their time to the organization if they find it worth their while. Else, they just move on to something else. The organization's values, vision and purpose play a role in their choice of company to work for. The workforce is more diverse, which creates a greater need for inclusion and bringing women and minorities into leadership roles.

Santosh Iyer, MD and CEO of Mercedes-Benz India, feels that it is not easy to manage multigenerational talent and balance diverse needs. Organizations need to create and harmonize policies and processes that account for this diversity.

There is also an increase in the thinking of 'living for the now'. The concept of building a career over a period of time, or the concept of saving for later, is also reducing. Young professionals are happy to move from one gig to another and even take a break between jobs to travel and experience life.

Anusha Shetty, CEO of Grey India, works with a large Gen Z population. She says, 'They have a different approach to work. They ask questions and have opinions, and leaders need to be able to deal with that.'

Moonlighting is another concept that has been gaining traction in certain industries. Leaders need to have an open mind to understand the implications of these challenges and how to deal with them to continue to deliver results.

Managing people across cultures is also a challenge. There are different career drivers in different parts of the world. Many leaders who have worked across cultures need to adapt to cultural norms and requirements. **Nitish Kapoor, president, Emerging Markets at Reckitt,** who has worked across four continents, feels that cultural and situational agility is critical for leaders as they take on new challenges. He says, 'It is very important to listen to local and emerging expertise, and build a team with capabilities that the leader may not have themselves.'

Personal challenges

A leader is also a human being with his/her own set of challenges. Leaders also need to manage their personal world outside of work. There are challenges that need to be tackled on a daily basis, crises to be managed and problems to be solved away from work. The fact that boundaries have blurred between home and work and personal and professional causes more challenges in this hyperconnected world.

In his book, *Three Levels of Leadership*,[7] James Scouller talks about public (leading a team), private (leading individuals) and personal (leading yourself) leadership. In order to succeed at the outer levels of leadership, a leader must succeed at the inner level, especially at the level of self-mastery.

Vivek Gambhir, ex-CEO GCPL and Partner, Lightspeed Ventures, says finding ways to fuel yourself is a challenge. 'You have to bring your authentic self to work. You need to bring compassion into leadership. You need to manage your energies.'

Amrita Randhawa, CEO of Publicis Groupe, Asia Pacific, communicated proactively to her ex-company when she was going through a personal challenge and needed the support of the team to manage that. **Gabriel Fernandez, president, emerging markets at Mars Wrigley,** feels that if he does not prioritize and solve personal challenges, it will impact his leadership at other levels.

Managing family responsibilities

Indra Nooyi, in her book, *My Life in Full*,[8] has shared the challenges she faced while bringing up her daughters and managing a full-time role. She has spoken about the guilt of missing out on 'coffee mornings' at her children's school and the strategies she had to deploy to manage her personal life even as she succeeded in her career.

Lack of adequate childcare impacts many women leaders who are either stressed and burnt out at work or drop out of the leadership journey because it is too hard to manage both. More than 3 million women dropped out of the workforce in the USA because of a lack of childcare support, impacting their career and leadership aspirations.[9]

Decisions from our personal lives impact our careers and vice versa. Ratan Tata has shared that he was well settled and employed in the USA but came back to India because his grandmother wanted him back. **Sathya Sriram, former CEO of Preventive Care, Apollo Hospitals and Vignesh Nandakumar, CEO of Enfinity Global,** worked in the USA but moved back to Chennai to be closer to family.

Another leader shared that he did not take up a posting abroad because of ageing parents who were his responsibility. Many women leaders have shifted careers because of a spouse's move.

Stable and supportive relationships with a spouse can be a huge benefit for a corporate career, especially for leaders in high-profile jobs. Many of the leaders we spoke to credit their partner's constant support for being able to do their job well. Sustaining this critical relationship is extremely important.

Marital conflicts and divorces are costly, both financially and mentally. The Bill and Melinda Gates Foundation, which was managed by both of them, faced leadership and strategic uncertainties after their divorce.

In her book, *Couples that Work*,[10] Jennifer Petriglieri speaks about the three stages of life where couples actively need to manage their career and relationships.

1. Achieving interdependence: In their twenties and thirties, couples need to navigate parenthood and career ambitions and move from having independent careers to interdependent careers.

2. Transitioning to a new path: In their forties, couples wrestle with what they really want once the active childcare responsibilities reduce. This is also the time when one of the couples can be on a path to greater growth and ambition while another may want different things out of life. If one partner wants to be in a senior leadership role, another may take a step back to allow for this.
3. Exploring new horizons: In their sixties, post-retirement, couples need to redefine identities, grapple with failing health, care giving for aged parents and also enjoy the rewards of greater financial freedom and reduction in career stress. Again, if one spouse wants to pursue a completely different path of social engagement and active contribution and another wants a quiet life, there can be strife and stress on the personal front.

Leaders lead busy lives with hectic schedules, frequent travel and added responsibilities. Actively managing the important relationships in their lives and being there in times of need for their loved ones can become a challenge.

Managing personal well-being

Time is a precious commodity for senior leaders. One of the things that falls behind is personal health and well-being. Leaders need to ensure that they manage their time and priorities in a way that gives them time to manage their own well-being.

Kedar Lele, CEO of Castrol, admits, 'There is a lot to do and I end up doing my duty, versus doing what I love. As a CEO, I am empowered, but there are many stakeholders pulling in different directions. My well-being does get compromised.'

Personal well-being also includes the importance of being aware of their own self-limiting beliefs and mindsets that can keep them from growing as a leader. Managing the inner game is critical to mastering the outer game. Tim Gallwey talks about the importance of managing this internal chatter in his book *The Inner Game of Work*.[11] Unilever's leadership model[12] emphasizes the importance of the inner game, which includes a sense of purpose and managing emotions and intellect. Leaders who are very caught up in the outer game find it challenging to pause, reflect and calibrate. This, in turn, prevents personal growth and learning that are necessary to play the outer game well.

Managing personal crises

A sickness, a divorce, bereavement, children's illness, spouse's career moves—many of these are distracting at their best and daunting at their worst. Leaders wear multiple other hats and straddle multiple worlds.

When I (Nirupama) was a director with AchieveGlobal India, leading the profit centre and a team of consultants, I was also a new mother with an infant daughter. When the nanny who looked after our baby fell ill, followed by my baby falling sick, I had to navigate the crisis along with the job. Though my manager and work environment were supportive, it still took a huge toll on me. Rajesh also had to take leave from his job to tide over the situation. Finally, I took a call to take a break from work because of the stress and guilt of not being able to do justice to my roles as a mother and as a leader.

Another leader could not take up a lucrative role in a different city because his autistic child had the best care and support system in their current location. A senior leader coached by Nirupama faced a dilemma because her spouse had been offered a long-coveted job move overseas. She could not focus on her job responsibilities because of the stress of making the right decision for her career and the family.

While many such challenges make us strong, more resilient, empathetic and tougher in the long run, they can be very difficult to manage in the moment along with the leadership responsibilities.

Across all categories, there were some common aspects about the nature of the challenges. All challenges were adaptive in nature. Apart from that, three things stood out.

Pace—too many things are changing too quickly

Many of the leaders we spoke to emphasized the old adage—'Change is the only constant'. While change is a part of life, the pace of change has never been so fast. Before one change has been managed, another one shoots out at you. The Covid-19 years forced rapid and massive change across industries.

One big area of rapid change in recent times has been in technology and this got further amplified during and after the pandemic. During a talk to report the numbers in 2020, Microsoft CEO Satya Nadella said, 'We have seen two years of digital transformation in two months!'

Madhav Kalyan, MD and head of payments, Asia Pacific, JP Morgan, says, 'The rapid change in technology has a far-reaching impact on the financial services industry, and leaders need to be well-versed with the changing realities.' Digital disruption cuts across industries, and the leader who is not on top of it will be left behind.

Social media forces marketers to respond immediately to topically leverage a new viral trend or the latest sensation. The influencer who was so impactful two months ago is no longer viable as an endorser.

Staying relevant is a key challenge articulated by many leaders. According to **Debjani Ghosh, former president of NASSCOM**, 'In today's fast-paced world, leaders have to deal with the danger of becoming redundant. Sometimes, the leaders' ego prevents them from adapting to this rapid change.'

Rahul Shankar, group CEO, Quest Retail and former CEO of Modicare, says, 'When we start growing exponentially, the rest of the organization sometimes struggles to keep pace. This is where the leader needs to step in to ensure that all functions of the organization are firing on all cylinders to fuel the momentum.'

Pervasiveness—everything is connected

When a plane crashed into the World Trade Center in New York in September 2011, it set off shock waves, the impact of which is still being felt today. Covid-19 was just a virus infection in China before it changed the world. Challenges are viral in their spread and reach.

The challenges cut across functions and domains. The interconnectedness of businesses and systems today implies that there will be a ripple effect of one challenge across many areas. Communication cannot be contained, and small acts can have large consequences.

A process change in the factory will impact the environment, which will impact the brand image, which, in turn, will impact the share price very quickly.

Predictability—nothing is certain

Even as we have the ability to process more information than ever before, even though we have plenty of data, it does not help to predict the future. No one can predict where the next disruptive change will come from and how it will impact you. Despite all the data on exit polls and opinion polls, the final outcome of the elections has never been 100 per cent accurate.

When a war in one region seems to be dying down, another erupts in a different part of the world. We think that Covid-19 has ended, but we cannot predict the next outbreak. Competition can come from completely unexpected sources. **Suresh Narayanan, chairman and MD of Nestlé India,** says, 'Leaders need to be agile and adaptable in a volatile context so that they are able to navigate multifarious elements in a continuously changing environment with dexterity, trust and transparency.'

It is difficult to predict the domino effect on a business of a seemingly unconnected event that is happening thousands of miles away. The butterfly effect—a small change that can cause a compounding cascading effect—is in full force in today's interconnected world. An unforeseen event in one of the company's locations will cause the global share prices to fall almost immediately.

Amit Syngle, MD of Asian Paints, says that the most important aspect of a leader's role is to provide some semblance of certainty during uncertain times. **Saugata Gupta** adds, 'Managing a business is no longer like a game of golf; it has now become like a contact sport. There is no sanctity to annual operating plans; anything can happen anytime. We are starting to move to quarterly operating plans.'

It is also difficult to predict changes in our personal lives. We cannot foresee an illness, an accident, a lawsuit or a lottery. Things can and do change in an instant.

Imagine you are the leader facing these challenges. It is almost like facing a tennis ball machine that spits out balls at you at a rapid pace in all directions. Now, have multiple machines doing the same thing around you, each at a different pace and with a different kind of ball. Now, as some machines finish their quota of balls, new machines appear around you, spitting newer balls that look nothing like the typical tennis balls you were used to. All you have in your hands is a good old tennis racquet! Only a superhuman would be able to handle this situation.

The ability and the energy required to handle these challenges take a huge toll on the leader's well-being. Leaders who cannot manage the inner game cannot be effective in the outer game of leading others. Leaders who cannot create a supportive high performing team cannot handle the challenges on their own and will find themselves depleted, isolated and burnt out.

2

The Importance of Nurturing Leadership

'When we strive to become better than we are, everything around us becomes better too.'

—Paulo Coelho

Jacinda Ardern, the former prime minister of New Zealand, resigned in January 2023, citing occupational burnout as the main reason for her to step back from her leadership role. In an emotional speech, she said, 'I am leaving because with such a privileged role comes responsibility, the responsibility to know when you are the right person to lead, and also when you are not. I know what this job takes, and I know that I no longer have enough in the tank to do it justice. It is that simple.'[13]

Being a CEO comes with power and perks, but it is also a lonely and stressful job. One CEO expressed her role as 'a lonely satellite in its own orbit'. Many top leaders feel the weight of their huge responsibility—to the employees, customers, shareholders and regulators. There is pressure to perform and deliver results quickly while ensuring that the organization branding and reputation are maintained.

Boards of large organizations are less shy about CEO dismissals. Some 15 per cent of the 2023 CEO exits tracked by Spencer Stuart were forced dismissals, well above the rate of the last few years but in line with historical averages.

A study by Harvard Law[14] shows that the average CEO tenure is declining. The median tenure among the S&P 500 companies has decreased 20 per cent from six years in 2013 to four years and nine and a half months in 2022. According to the research, the declining tenure rates continue to reflect the challenges CEOs currently face, and their ability to navigate these changes and drive sustainable growth remains vital in shaping today's competitive business environment.

Not all leaders may be as candid as Jacinda Ardern, but stress and burnout are natural for those who are in a position of responsibility. An article in CEO *Coaching International* found that stress was the silent CEO killer of top-performing leaders.[15] A 2021 study of 1600 CEOs by the National Bureau of Economic Research called 'CEO Stress, Aging and Death'[16] found that stress caused by industry distress reduced a CEO's lifespan by 18 months. An analysis of photos of CEOs during an industrial, economic or financial crisis showed signs of visible ageing brought on by stress.

A 2018 study, 'CEOs, a Personal Reflection',[17] by global search firm Egon Zehnder of 405 CEOs including forty-four CEOs from India, found that 41 per cent of CEOs found it difficult to manage family and personal life, while 34 per cent struggled to manage their stress levels. Only 27 per cent of CEOs felt fully prepared for their current role.

Christina Maslach, a pioneer researcher on the subject at the University of California, Berkeley, says that burnout refers to a syndrome of emotional exhaustion and cynicism that frequently occurs among people who do 'people work'.[18] People suffering from burnout generally have these identifiable characteristics: (1) chronic fatigue; (2) anger at those making demands; (3) self-criticism for putting up with the demands; (4) cynicism, negativity and irritability; (5) a sense of being besieged and (6) hair-trigger display of emotions.

A leader who was being coached by Nirupama admitted to feeling stressed but was unable to express it to others. 'The CEO cannot afford to be emotional, but I find myself shouting at people even when it is not necessary.' Leaders are under pressure to put on a brave face and demonstrate optimism and courage even if they feel drained and depleted. **Ritesh Gauba** admits, 'If I look sad or less energetic, it affects the morale of others. It can have a ripple effect.'

Meenakshi Nevatia, MD of Pfizer, echoes this: 'There is no off day. Your energy needs to be high all the time. You need to show up for every meeting with the right energy.' **Dr Parag Rindani** works in an industry where the wrong decision can cost a human life. There is a lot of stress because the stakes are high. In his early days, heading a hospital, Dr Rindani hardly took any leave for a few years.

'CEOs are quite tired,' says Jason Baumgarten, head of the global CEO and boards practice at executive firm Spencer Stuart, quoted in a *Fortune* magazine article.[19] 'They've been waiting for a calm period to transition and thought there'd be one post-Covid-19, but of course we fell into high inflation and macroeconomic instability.'

Sudhir Sitapati, CEO and MD, GCPL, says that anticipating change in a very dynamic environment is a key challenge for CEOs. The daily challenges that he encounters at work lead to stress, which then manifests both physically and mentally.

While there is never a dull moment in a CEO's life, the rapid, unbridled pace of change and complexity of the role takes its toll. It takes a toll on the health of the leader and shows up as heart attacks, hypertension, blood pressure, ulcers and chronic fatigue. It takes a toll on mental and emotional health. A survey by Deloitte in 2022[20] also found that one in three C-suite executives constantly struggles with fatigue and poor mental health. As many as 70 per cent have considered quitting their jobs to try to reset their emotional balance.

'Being agile takes up a lot of energy. Burnout is an issue. Good performance requires you to be switched on all the time,' says **Radhika Piramal, executive director at VIP Industries**.

Harish Devarajan, leadership coach and transformation consultant, says, 'Leadership is like the flywheel in the organizational motor. The quality of leadership impacts the overall effectiveness of the organization. In the current and emerging context, when we are bound to witness a quicker ascent of talent to leadership roles, the significance of leadership development assumes even greater importance.'

Pramath Sinha, who has helped set up institutions such as ISB (Indian School of Business), Ashoka University and Vedica Scholars Programme, has groomed many leaders and seen them in action. 'There are different ways in which leaders deal with challenges. Those who cannot handle challenges well either get very stressed or resign. I have seen very smart people, who have the right education and experience, tripping up because they have no idea how to deal with new challenges. Your past successes do not prepare you for your next failure.'

The challenges also take a toll on relationships within and outside the organization. Many CEOs feel that they do not give enough time to their family or friends even though they see this as important. It is easy for the CEO to become stuck in a vicious cycle of constant work where they are unable to get off the treadmill to recharge themselves. The corporate work culture has also made it difficult for leaders to seem human, vulnerable and in need of support. Apart from work pressure, the leader is under pressure to project a confident, calm and competent image. While everyone claims that they need to be authentic leaders, the system looks down upon anything that can be construed as weak.

Nirupama was coaching a new CEO who approached her at a personal level. He did not want the organization to sponsor the coaching sessions since it might send a signal that he was not ready for the job. It is difficult for CEOs to admit that they need a coach, a therapist or a counsellor for fear of being seen as unfit for the job.

Without support from outside, depleted of internal resources, the CEO can face a huge struggle to stay afloat and manage the barrage of challenges. **Nisaba Godrej, executive chairperson of Godrej Consumer Products Limited (GPCL)**, says, 'The ego and introversion are barriers to showing up in the way you need to. If you have the privilege of leadership, you also have the responsibility to show up as your best self every time.'

Puneet Chandok, president of Microsoft India and South Asia, constantly reminds himself that he needs to nurture himself. 'I can't pour from an empty cup. No amount of success at work is worth a failure at home.'

Sameer Wadhawan, ex-CHRO, Samsung India, adds, 'Leaders need to take care of themselves first before they take care of others. They need to create space to cut off from the noise and get some me-time to reflect. It is important to create routines and rituals around me-time. A ritual that I still follow is my me-time during my 11 a.m. coffee.'

AI and machines might seem like a reality of the future, but humans are all still creatures of nature. A plant, animal or child can grow only if provided with the right care and sustenance. The plant or child needs to be fed, tended to and protected from danger if it has to live to its full potential.

Nature requires nurturing

The words nurturing and leadership have never been used together. The act of nurturing is seen as feminine, synonymous with caregiving, which has never been associated with the more masculine act of leading others. Leadership, as we know it, has been about setting tough goals, meeting stiff targets, beating the competition and galvanizing the team to achieve the objectives against all odds.

The drive for results cannot go away. A leader needs to have the functional competencies and task orientation to get the job done. But that alone is not enough!

In fact, the constantly changing environment and demands from multiple stakeholders put an inordinate amount of pressure on the leader, who often ends up taking shortcuts and sacrificing personal and employee well-being in the pursuit of profits. Growth cannot be forced. Injecting steroids can show you short-term success, but it is not sustainable in the long run.

Leaders need to be nurturers. The leader who can provide care, protection and resources for growth will build a robust organization where everyone can perform at their full potential. **Pavan Bhatia, ex CHRO at AMENA in**

PepsiCo says, 'Nurturing leadership is not about return on investments (ROI). It's about return on invested emotions (ROIE). Leaders who nurture themselves and others will deliver sustainable results in this VUCA and increasingly AI-led world.'

Deepak Jayaraman, author of *Play to Potential*, sums it up well. He says, 'Given the ask from leadership today, it has become imperative that leaders nurture themselves in order to be effective in their roles. Three reasons come to mind. Firstly, nurturing oneself in the simplest of terms is about keeping adequate "gas in the tank" as you go about your role. Nourishment and replenishment are a key part of the equation if one is keen to play the long game and build to last. Secondly, leaders need to bring a healthy level of head and heart in their roles. Given the volatility around them, it has become that much more important for leaders to tune into their instinct, and that requires deliberate nurturing. Thirdly, the paradigm of leadership is moving towards inspiring by who you are "being" rather than what you are "doing". And that requires leadership to show up in a certain way, which once again requires inner work and nourishing the heart and the soul for the leader to come across as authentic.'

A leader today is not a general marshalling his troops to win a battle. Leaders are more like gardeners. While the analogy of leaders as gardeners is not new, we believe that the work of creating a wonderful garden starts with the gardener.

We have a small balcony garden in our home, and a gardener comes weekly to tend to it. The gardener we had earlier was a surly fellow called Bharat who seemed knowledgeable but disinterested in our garden. He was irregular in his visits, unclear in his instructions about tending to the plants and did not seem to care about my dying curry leaves or limp petunias. It was a job he did reluctantly. We changed the gardener. The current one, Ram Baran, is pleasant, punctual and proactive. He knows which are indoor plants and which ones need more light, and he also tells me the frequency and amount of watering each plant needs. He is just as happy as I am when the little red chillies appear in the chilli plant. We feel the difference.

Nurturing builds the necessary resilience to handle the multiple challenges that a leader faces. In their book, *Building Resilience for Success: A Resource for Managers and Organizations*, Cary Cooper, Jill Flint Taylor and Michael Pern share four aspects of resilience: self confidence, adaptability, purpose and social support. All these aspects require a steady nurturing of your own resources and the creation of a supportive eco system. People who are well resourced, can deal with adversity and bounce back from challenges quickly.

So nurturing has to happen at two levels for any leader: **Nurturing the Self** and **Nurturing Others.** It has become ever more important for leaders in high-stress jobs who carry the responsibility for external shareholders and internal employees to take care of their physical, mental, emotional and spiritual well-being. Only if they do that can they support others.

Leaders cannot just hire the best talent; they need to provide an environment where talent can grow and thrive. A March 2015 BCG Report, *The Global Leadership and Talent Index*[21] found that companies that are rated highly on leadership and talent management capabilities—the 'talent magnets'—increased their revenue 2.2 times faster and profits 1.5 times faster than the 'talent laggards'.

Nurturing yourself and nurturing others go hand in hand. This needs to happen simultaneously and continuously. A leader who only takes care of his/her own needs cannot grow at scale. This leader will be unable to inspire and lead other people to achieve a larger goal. Even a talented artist who shines as an individual performer needs an entourage which makes her successful; a superstar athlete needs an entire team of coaches, nutritionists, physiotherapists, sponsors and mentors to enable her to compete at the highest level. This ecosystem needs to be nurtured for long term success. A leader who extends himself for others and neglects self-care, personal growth and learning or emotional well-being, cannot sustain this kind of leadership for long. Leaders who overestimate sacrifice and abnegation experience rapid burnout. Successful leaders who create impact at scale are well resourced and mindful about ensuring that they bring their best game to work.

In the following chapters, we will examine how over 115 CEOs from the corporate world and outside nurture themselves and others. We share stories and best practices of how this nurturing can be done mindfully, strategically and in a holistic manner. We hope that new and emerging leaders will find useful information, interesting insights and motivational inspiration from the stories, best practices and research that we share in this book.

Understand your Nurturing Quotient

Before we embark on any journey, it is always good to do a self-audit to see where we are on that journey. This helps us get a sense of awareness of our current state so that we can plan out the future state and work towards it in the most effective and efficient manner.

In this regard, we have designed a simple assessment tool that will give you an initial diagnosis to find out your own **Nurturing Quotient (NQ)**. This tool will help you take an honest look at your current nurturing practices across all the domains of nurturing the self and others and provide you with a great starting point.

The results of the assessment can then be used by you to plot your future course of action in a more structured and mindful way. This could include continuing with the best practices that you are already doing in certain domains and building new practices in the ones where you currently under-index.

Scan this QR code to access the questionnaire.

Section II

Growing the Self

3

Nurture the Self

'Self-love, my liege, is not so vile a sin, as self-neglecting.'

—William Shakespeare, *Henry V*

In order for us to be able to perform to our potential, we need to nurture ourselves in a holistic manner. In this chapter, we will examine nurturing ourselves across four domains: **body**, **mind**, **heart** and **soul**. There are, of course, overlaps between the four domains, as each one impacts the other. Yet there are clear distinctions between the way we nurture each aspect of ourselves.

NURTURING SELF

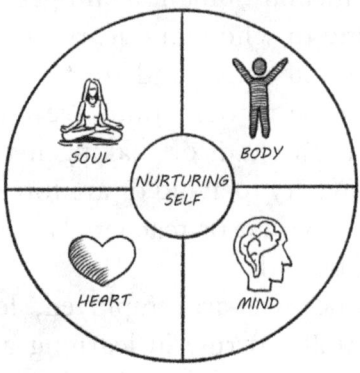

Body: This is the physical domain, which refers to the growth and well-being of the body. Physical well-being is easily observable and measurable in terms of height, weight, BMI, blood pressure and several other markers. At the childhood stage, we track and measure the growth and change in the physical domain frequently and clearly. The growth in centimetres of a child is tracked through pencil marks on a wall, clothes are outgrown and replaced frequently and there are regular visits to the paediatrician. At adulthood, it is more about sustenance and maintenance.

In the absence of a parent taking care of our physical markers, we need to be more mindful and careful about nurturing this domain. Often it gets neglected. We feel that we have reached our maximum or optimum growth stage and leave the rest to fate! During the early years of the career, there is more focus on doing well at work, finding a romantic partner and living 'your best life' before settling down. The following decade of the thirties is spent climbing the career ladder and managing family. Time is a scarce commodity. When people become senior leaders in their forties and fifties, they have to unlearn the habits of their youth and start focusing actively on the body.

Mind: The mental domain again gets greater focus in childhood. Going to school and learning new things every day keeps the mind active and fresh. Frequent tests and exams give exercise to our brain. We are spurred on by goals of passing an exam or making it through rigorous job interviews. We try to avoid or are forced to avoid other distractions by a parent or teacher. There is time devoted to learning and growth.

However, once we are employed, learning is more organic. The 70-20-10 rule in learning and development says that 70 per cent of learning happens on the job,

20 per cent through interpersonal interactions and 10 per cent through formal training. The early days in any new role are full of learning, and we are forced to stay on our toes. Once employees reach a senior level, most of their time is spent directing others, problem-solving or managing stakeholders to get alignment. Others may find a comfort zone and choose to stay in it, inadvertently avoiding learning opportunities. Leaders can be learners only if they learn to keep their minds sharp and active.

Heart: The mental and emotional domains are closely connected, but there are significant differences in the way we deal with them. The emotional domain is one we often take for granted. Our emotional mould is created in childhood. Our experiences as a child, along with our nature, shapes how we express and deal with emotions. Children who grow up in loving households with a nurturing family have an innate sense of emotional well-being. Children who are encouraged to express their feelings and receive the emotions of others with grace and compassion become emotionally intelligent adults.

Research suggests that our mental health, which encompasses many emotional issues, is declining. The Mental State of India 2024[22] report from the Observer Research Foundation suggests that the mental well-being in the country is lower in 2023 than it was in 2020 and that mental health was worsening, especially for the youths between the ages of eighteen and twenty-four. While it is difficult to quantify India's mental health problem in the absence of recent data, it is clear that the burden of mental health problems is on the rise in the country. It is critical that we become proactive about managing the emotional domain as adults.

Soul: The world of profit and loss is often portrayed as a soulless, bloodsucking hellhole, devoid of deep noble emotions and human connections. Charlie Chaplin's classic film *Modern Times*, a dark comedy set in the 1930s, shows the exploitation of workers and portrays the employee as just a cog in the wheel. More recent films such as *Wall Street* again show the greedy, grasping nature of the capitalist system, which dehumanizes people and brings out the worst in them. Competition is usually unhealthy, and combativeness is prized over compromise.

Yet, many inspirational leaders across the world who have created transformations and led nations, like the Dalai Lama, Nelson Mandela, Bishop Desmond Tutu or Mahatma Gandhi, have had deep spiritual connections which enabled them to lead at scale.

The spiritual domain is one that is not usually addressed actively in the working world. Some people do have a calling or a sense of purpose from an early age. Others grow up with strong faith-based practices, inherited from parents and the community. Many people do find contribution and fulfilment in their work, but they need to work at it.

A leader could be strong on the physical domain through high-impact exercises, but she could ignore the spiritual domain. Another leader could have multiple nurturing hobbies like gardening or cooking but unconsciously neglect the mental domain because he does not keep time aside for new learning.

An activity like yoga can nurture a person across all four domains. **Ira Trivedi, Yog Love founder** and acclaimed author, says, 'The world that we live in today and the lifestyle that we lead put a lot of strain on the mind and body. The lack of enough physical mobility, the overdose of social media and the pollution in the environment further add to the strain. As a leader, one needs to be in a state of balance so that you can reflect that balance on others as well. Yoga is a holistic practice that can help create this balance across all four dimensions of energy.

Yoga helps one nurture themselves physically through the various asanas. It also helps in nurturing oneself mentally because it has been scientifically proven that yoga helps relax your nervous system, and one is able to think better and have more creative thoughts. Yoga calms one down and gets them into a state of emotional equilibrium, which facilitates better decision making and being more balanced with your emotions.'

Many leaders spoke about their passion for golf, which also satisfies mental needs of focus and mindfulness along with emotional needs of connecting with fellow golfers on the course. **Amit Jain, chairman, Sanofi CHC and Collective Newsroom,** says, 'Golf helps me focus and connect with nature. When I am playing golf, I am only thinking about the next shot and about optimizing course management. It also helps me build new connections and gives me a great insight into my playing partner. The sport gives me a perspective on life and leadership. It teaches me that I cannot control everything. Some days are good and some are very challenging. I need to be resilient and have great equanimity regardless of the circumstances.'

Research from the Greater Good Science Center, University of California, Berkeley, shows that having a sense of purpose has positive effects on all other aspects.[23] People with a strong sense of purpose had better cognitive functioning, less stress, better health and longevity. In a 2019 study by Anne Colby and colleagues at Stanford University, they surveyed almost 1200 Americans in their midlife about their well-being and what goals were important to them. The researchers found significantly higher well-being among people who were involved in pursuing beyond-the-self goals, compared to those who were pursuing other types of goals.

Being a member of a book club helps to not only nurture the mental domain through reading but the connection with other members also supports our emotional well-being. Similarly, being a part of a spiritual group or volunteering for a cause with the family also enriches the soul, along with deepening emotional bonds. Running a marathon with your running group to raise money for a good cause and enjoying the hours of mindful focus while you run help you score well on all four dimensions of nurturing the self.

Nurturing the self does not require additional time or effort. **Sanjiv Mehta** believes that it is important to allocate time wisely to the right priorities. He nurtures himself through his daily routine. 'I get up at 5 a.m., make my tea, watch the sunrise, read the newspaper, reach office early, plan well, fix the agenda to make my meetings more efficient and effective and invest time in performance management, capability building and in nurturing people. I also eat well and sleep for seven hours.'

However we approach it, nurturing the self has many components. It is important for leaders to regularly nurture themselves in one or more domains of energy. This helps in restoring their energy equilibrium and enables them to lead a holistic and well-balanced life. In the following chapters, we examine each of these in more detail.

4

Nourish Your Body

'Take care of your body, it is the only place you have to live.'

—Jim Rohn

A typical post-pandemic workday for a leader can be a series of virtual meetings, often at odd hours because of global calls with multiple time zones. The leader may not have time for regular meals or rest. A good night's sleep becomes a luxury. Many leaders who travel across time zones feel the added burden of red-eye flights and travel fatigue. And on top of all of this, leaders need to manage the diverse needs of multiple stakeholders in an increasingly volatile and dynamic environment. All of this takes a toll on their health and well-being, and prevents them from operating at their full potential. This ultimately impacts their leadership and the business.

In a decade-long study of 1500 executives, Limbach and Sonnenburg (2015)[24] demonstrated that a CEO's physical fitness is associated with higher firm profitability and higher M&A announcement returns, in line with other known benefits of physical fitness such as stress management, cognitive functioning and overall job performance.[25]

Good physical well-being is the foundation of our overall well-being. The vagaries of this VUCA world create a lot of negative energy for leaders. In their quest to do their job effectively, many leaders compromise on their health and well-being.

The lack of an appropriate lifestyle routine impacts our physical well-being. Leaders need to find ways to nurture their physical energy to ensure physical well-being. Physical well-being is about our ability to maintain a healthy and holistic life where we are able to carry out our daily activities without any fatigue or physical discomfort. It refers to the quality of the physical state of our body—our weight, posture, the health of our organs and the absence of any ailments or illnesses. Physical well-being is also about having the right amount of energy to effectively deal with things that come our way.

In his pathbreaking book *Outlive*,[26] Dr Peter Attia talks about longevity having two components: lifespan and health span. Lifespan is about how long we live—our chronological age. Health span is how well we live—the quality of our years. Health span is about ensuring our overall well-being so that we can perform our work effectively and efficiently.

Leaders who are aware of the need for physical well-being and actively work towards it have more energy, are better at decision-making and enhance overall performance. **Sivakumar Sundaram, CEO of Bennett Coleman & Co. Ltd,** says, 'Running opens up my mind; it allows for fresh thoughts and fresh energy; it allows me to be with myself. When I am thinking of a problem, by the time I finish my run, I am likely to have a couple of solutions.'

The leader's physical well-being can also be contagious. When a leader prioritizes their physical well-being, they often serve as role models for others in the organization. Leaders can thus create a positive cascading impact on the physical well-being across the organization leading to better performance and engagement. Says **Ritesh Gauba** 'I am passionate about physical fitness and I actively propagate this with my friends and colleagues and it has rubbed off on them as well.'

Hemant Malik, executive director, ITC Limited, believes that it is in the organization's interest to be healthy. 'We created and used FUROFIT to motivate people to become fit. People were divided into teams. They could do a max of 15,000 steps a day and get points for steps. There were at least 100 people who were doing 15,000 steps a day. Lots of people have lost weight and become fitter. The target has since been increased to 16,500 steps a day, and many people continue this beyond the programme.'

Anupriya Acharya, CEO of Publicis Groupe, South Asia, talks about the interesting initiative that they launched in her organization. 'We launched an initiative called Pubfit in 2021 to help people to stay fit. We tied up with Dr Marcus Ranney of Human Edge and used the five pillars of well-being and longevity to inspire people to be the best version of themselves,' she says.

These initiatives help in building positive peer pressure and create interest in physical well-being.

Leaders who are physically fit are also able to manage stress effectively. They also don't end up passing on the stress in the organization, and this helps maintain employee morale. The physical well-being of leaders also builds their mental and emotional resilience. This helps leaders to overcome obstacles, persevere in the face of adversity and inspire their teams to do their best, thus enhancing the overall quality of excellence in the organization. Despite the established linkages between the physical well-being of leaders and organizational performance and engagement, it is not an area of focus for many leaders. Leaders are still warming up to the idea that it is important for them to take care of their physical well-being. They are slowly realizing that this is the foundation on which they can then build their mental, emotional and spiritual well-being, thus enabling them to lead a holistic well-balanced life. This will allow leaders to effectively and holistically nurture themselves and act as role models so that they can positively impact and inspire those around them.

Vice Admiral Anil Kumar Chawla, who has retired from the Indian Navy, says, 'Health comes first. I do yoga regularly, go for long walks and play golf.'

Anuradha Acharya, founder and CEO of Ocimum Bio Solutions and MapmyGenome, feels that there is a lot more awareness about health and well-being now. Since she is in the business of preventive health, she is particular about tracking her glucose indicators, heart rate and stress levels. She wears an Oura Ring, which gives a round-the-clock indication of sleep, stress and fitness levels. She advocates periodic testing, becoming aware of genetic markers for health risks and taking a proactive approach to managing health. Earlier, she used to be proud of the fact that she could do with three to four hours of sleep, but now she prioritizes at least six and a half to seven hours of good rest to feel recharged for the next day.

There are three key aspects that impact our physical well-being. These are ensuring regular and adequate physical exercise, having the right nutrition and hydration and getting the right amount and quality of sleep. We will examine each of them in some detail along with the interplay between them.

Physical exercise

The phrase 'rest and relaxation' is an often-used cliché. While resting can be relaxing, physical exercise can also lead to us relaxing, reducing our stress levels and improving our overall well-being. Physical exercise has the ability to exhilarate and relax, it can stimulate and calm, it can counter depression and alleviate stress.

Physical exercise has some direct stress-busting benefits, and this has a neurochemical basis. Studies have shown that aerobic exercise reduces the levels of stress hormones such as adrenaline and cortisol. It also stimulates the production of endorphins, which is the brain's feel-good neurotransmitter, which acts as a natural painkiller and also improves our ability to sleep, which in turn reduces stress. Endorphins also naturally help improve mood, cognition and concentration, leading to mental and emotional well-being.

I (**Rajesh**) am very passionate about my fitness regime. 'I ensure that I do at least thirty minutes of physical activity every day. My usual routine when I am not travelling is seventy-five minutes of yoga every weekday morning and sixty minutes of gym every alternate evening, with some walking thrown in. When I am travelling, I always carry my walking shoes with me. I also try to find a way to practice yoga even while I am travelling. I keep track of my fitness regime through an Excel spreadsheet with a red mark for a day of inactivity. I have had about twenty-five inactive days since 2018.'

Nirupama is also a regular yoga practitioner and enjoys walking outdoors. She took up running at the age of fifty and tries to run 5–10 km every week. She also does her self-paced Pilates workout and strength training twice a week with a personal trainer. **Kalpesh Parmar, regional general manager of Mars Wrigley,** likes to mix it up. He says, 'I do a mix of weight training, walking, playing badminton, cycling and golf over the course of the week. I sleep on time and wake up early. I ensure that I get good nutrition and hydration through the day.'

Vineeta Singh, co-founder and CEO of SUGAR Cosmetics, is passionate about running. She says, 'Running is my meditation. I just focus on the breath and movement. It gives endorphins for the energy but also cuts down the noise. On the days I run, I am a better leader, partner and parent. It is a great antidepressant tool. I do about 100 km a month, with three to four runs a week, and I have now been doing it for sixteen years.'

Madhav Kalyan says, 'I like to do short-distance runs on most weekday mornings. This brings a sense of routine and discipline. Over weekends, I end up doing long-distance cycling and playing pickleball, which, apart from the physical activity, also helps me connect with like-minded people and makes me happy.'

Mohit Sadaani, co-founder, The Moms Co., does a lot of physical activities, which include going to the gym four to five times a week, some golf during the week and regular walks. **Jagrut Kotecha, CEO of PepsiCo India and South Asia,** says, 'I try and run 5 km every day; it is my me-time. I have been playing golf for the last twenty years. Apart from the physical activity and being with nature, it has taught me resilience.'

Physical exercise has several dimensions to it including muscle strengthening, building stamina, improving flexibility, developing balance and enhancing cardiovascular endurance. We need all of these to different extents depending on our starting point. It is important to understand these aspects well and then determine which ones we want to focus on depending on our personal goals.

Pranab Barua, who is on the board of Nykaa, says, 'I find playing sports to be entertaining as well as beneficial both mentally and physically. I always had a sport that I was serious about at various stages of my life: football and athletics in school and college, squash till my fifties and golf thereafter. I also do some core exercises and weight training to keep myself fit.'

Toshan Tamhane, global COO of UPL, is a keen trekker. 'I have been on several treks across the world, including the Himalayas, the Alps, Mount Kilimanjaro, Mount Elbrus and so on. These help me work towards a goal and stay fit. For me, fitness is not an option but a necessity. I do some exercise every day even if it is some bodywork in my hotel room after a long flight.'

Manu Anand, former president, Mondelēz AMEA and ex-CEO PepsiCo India, says, 'I have started enjoying trekking. Apart from the physical activity and connect with nature, I get to meet interesting people. It tests both physical abilities and mental toughness and encourages teamwork and looking out for each other.'

Aerobic exercise for twenty to thirty minutes at least three to four times a week can have a significant impact on our physical well-being. It is therefore important to have a physical exercise routine for ourselves. This can be anything—walking, running, swimming, cycling, yoga, playing a sport or going to the gym. The important thing is to pick one or two physical activities that we enjoy and pursue them on a regular basis as part of our regular routine.

Examine your daily schedule and identify slots where you can seamlessly weave in a physical activity. **Puneet Davar, CEO of Tropilite Foods,** first ran to lose weight. He then ran an ultramarathon in Leh. Now, running is not just a routine but also a meditation. He runs almost 100 km every week, and it gives him great happiness.

Harsh Mariwala says, 'I exercise around 90 minutes every day, I like to mix it up. I do some weight training, yoga, swimming and Pilates. I also play golf thrice a week.'

The leaders who do not do physical activity on a daily basis use the weekends for some form of exercise, often combining it with the time they spend with family and friends. **Sandeep Kataria, global CEO of Bata,** who is based out of Lausanne, likes to go skiing over the weekend or play badminton.

Pankajam Sridevi, former MD of Commonwealth Bank, learnt swimming recently. This also helped her come out of her comfort zone and break the barrier of fear.

Gabriel Fernandez is into sports—he plays football and tennis and goes to the gym regularly. 'If I don't do this, I don't feel good. After exercise, I feel refreshed.' He has now taken up golf as well.

Neil George, former MD of Nivea and currently with Abbott Nutrition, is also a believer that 'what gets measured is what gets done'. He maintains a detailed 'Personal Goal' spreadsheet for all key activities, including regular medical check-ups, workouts, catch-up with friends, etc.

There are other collateral benefits of exercise as well. As our physical appearance improves, our waistline shrinks, our strength and stamina increase and our self-confidence and self-image improve. This can lead to a virtuous cycle of positivity of mind, body and heart. Playing a sport also gives us an opportunity to connect with like-minded people, make new friends and plug into their network, which enhances our sense of social well-being. All of these have a ripple effect on our overall well-being.

Nutrition and hydration

Physical well-being is not just about physical exercise. It is about doing things that positively impact our body, and it is also about avoiding things that negatively impact our body. One very important aspect of physical well-being is what we put into our bodies and what we don't. What we eat and drink has a profound impact on our health and well-being.

An unhealthy diet and irregular food habits can result in serious physical health complications, including obesity, heart disease and cancer. The WHO[27] states that eating a healthy diet, exercising and avoiding tobacco can prevent 80 per cent of type 2 diabetes cases and 40 per cent of cancers.

Physical exercise alone isn't enough for ensuring physical well-being. It is important to eat healthy and hydrate well. Eating healthy and eating right can have a myriad of benefits, including reducing obesity, strengthening muscles, improving memory, energizing the body, maintaining calmness and boosting the immune system.

Nutrition and diet are much-maligned words today. Everyone is talking about them, and there is so much literature on them. Dr Peter Attia, in his book *Outlive*,[28] breaks down nutrition into a few basic rules: don't eat too many calories or too few; consume sufficient protein and essential fats; obtain the vitamins and minerals you need and avoid pathogens and toxins. Being mindful of these rules and eating accordingly can have multiple short- and medium-term benefits on our health.

Today's leaders have a very demanding schedule. They end up working long hours, sometimes skipping meals, frequently travelling and attending many official dinners. All of these impact their nutritional intake and, in turn, impact their physical well-being. It is therefore very important for leaders to be mindful of the need for good nutrition and fit this into their routine.

Kavita Devgan, nutritionist and author of several books on nutrition, says, 'Let's admit it—we do eat wrong at work. That is unfortunate because we truly are what we eat. Most of us are at the office for the maximum number of waking hours on most days; what we eat at work is very important. But most employees do not get this connection. Companies that make policies do not understand how directly the health of their employees is related to their efficiency and thus the bottom line.'

Alpana Titus, GM of health and hygiene, Reckitt South East Asia, says, 'I have worked in the food industry, so I have a lot of awareness on this subject. I've been on a plant-based diet for a long time. I eat very little processed food. I prefer home-cooked meals, where primarily I have more control over the quality of the ingredients. I also practise intermittent fasting.'

The adage 'Eat breakfast like a king, lunch like a prince and dinner like a pauper' is attributed to Adelle Davis, a nutritionist and an author. Leaders would do well to draw inspiration from this. By following a proper eating time schedule along with the right type of foods we eat during the day, we can help ensure our physical health and mental well-being. Studies suggest that our body requires energy to sustain us throughout the day. And most importantly, the timing, along with what we eat, is essential to maintaining the flow of vitality. Eating the right meal at the right time can do wonders for our health and help us lead a well-balanced life.

After fasting for eight to twelve hours, when we wake up in the morning, our body requires a high glucose level that helps to maintain our energy level throughout the day.

This helps to energize us, improves our productivity and reduces stress. Having a healthy and hearty breakfast with food rich in fibre and protein helps us kickstart the day in the right manner.

Kedar Lele is very conscious about what he eats. He likes to mix it up a little—intermittent fasting and turning to a vegetarian diet help him to stay on top of his nutritional needs. **Vikas Chawla, MD and CEO, Compass Group, India**, says, 'I am maniacal about my fitness; I have a gym at home; I exercise at least three times a week. I am also a foodie—I love to eat, and hence I ensure I have adequate exercise to balance it out. These days, I am more mindful of what I eat and try to eat in moderation.'

Moderation is another key aspect of nutrition. *Hara hachi bu* is a Confucian teaching that instructs people to eat until they are 80 per cent full. The Japanese phrase translates to 'Eat until you are eight parts [out of ten] full.' Eating the right quantity is as important as eating well.

We, Rajesh and Nirupama, obtained a Food Intolerance profile, which gave an indication of foods to avoid. This helps to be more mindful of what we eat.

Hydrating right is an integral part of physical well-being and is very often ignored. About 60 per cent of an average adult body is water. Water plays several important roles in the body. It regulates our body temperature, it carries nutrients and oxygen to cells, it flushes out toxins from our body and it protects body organs and tissues.

Adequate hydration helps maximize physical performance. It has an impact on our strength, power and endurance. There are studies that show that the right levels of hydration aid in cognitive function and help improve mood. Dehydration can lead to fatigue, confusion and anxiety.

Being mindful of the amount of water we drink every day is key for our physical well-being. For men, it is generally recommended that they drink four litres of water per day, while for women, it is about three litres per day. It is important that we find our own hacks to ensure adequate hydration on a daily basis, which will go a long way in enhancing our physical well-being.

As **Kavita Devgan** says, 'The best way to keep a lid on non-communicable diseases and lifestyle diseases is to reform a captive audience—we are at our most captive at work, where we spend eight to ten hours a week.' Leaders who are mindful about nutrition also help to bring this focus to employees at work by offering healthy food at the cafeterias, replacing snacks with fruits and enabling employees to learn more about healthy eating.

Sleep

Mahatma Gandhi said, 'Each night, when I go to sleep, I die. And the next morning, when I wake up, I am reborn.' Sleep is a state of reduced physical and mental activity that allows our body to repair, refresh and rebuild. While we are sleeping, certain very important processes happen, including muscle repair, protein synthesis, hormone release and tissue growth. Sleep is also a powerful stress reliever, which improves concentration, regulates mood and sharpens judgement and decision-making.

CEOs like Bill Gates, Jeff Bezos and Elon Musk have spoken about changing their sleeping habits. Even Elon Musk, who boasted about pulling all-nighters and sleeping less than four hours daily, now feels the need to have six hours of sleep. 'Even though I'm awake more hours, I get less done. And the brain pain level is bad if I get less than six hours [of sleep],' Musk said in a 2024 CNBC interview.[29]

Lack of good sleep not only reduces mental clarity but also our ability to cope with stressful situations. There is increasing evidence that adequate, high-quality sleep can help prevent illnesses like respiratory infections, diabetes, heart disease and other serious conditions.

Leadership today tends to be a 24/7 job where leaders are constantly thinking about work. This can lead to mental fatigue and can have an adverse impact on our well-being. It is therefore important that leaders get an adequate amount of good quality sleep. Research has shown that people who are sleep deprived tend to underestimate its effects on them and attribute these effects to other issues.

When it comes to good sleep, both the quality and duration of sleep matter. There are many studies on how many hours of sleep are good for us, and there are various schools of thought on this. According to the Centers for Disease Control and Prevention (CDC),[30] adults aged between eighteen and sixty-nine need seven hours or more of sleep daily. This can, of course, change from one person to the other based on several factors, but six to eight hours of sleep seems to be a good target to aim towards.

The quality of sleep can be gauged by many indicators, including how quickly we fall asleep, how many times we wake up in the night, how many hours we sleep and how fresh we feel when we wake up in the morning.

In an ideal world, it is good to go to sleep early and wake up early, but that rarely happens because of our lifestyles. Even then, it is good to create some routine and discipline around our sleeping habits because of the profound impact that it can have on our overall well-being.

We (Nirupama and Rajesh) are particular about getting seven hours of sleep every night. Since we also wake up early in the morning for our yoga class, going to bed by 11 p.m. on weeknights is important. Rajesh likes to take a fifteen-minute nap during the day as well to recharge and refresh himself.

Nisaba Godrej says, 'Sleep is the bedrock of good health. Culturally, we tend to have bad sleeping habits. If you are not sleeping properly, it is a huge issue. I ensure that I get seven to eight hours of good sleep every night.'

Practising even some of these habits on a regular basis can improve the quality and duration of our sleep. **Uday Shankar** says, 'On weekdays, I sleep by 10 p.m. and wake up by 5.30 a.m. I then do my walk and my cardio exercises—this is my me-time. This energizes me and keeps me going for the day.'

Sandeep Sangwan, former MD of Castrol and CMO Castrol Global, ensures that he gets enough sleep—seven hours every night. 'I sleep by 11 p.m. and have a break of two hours between dinner and sleeping. I am far more effective the next day. Being physically active helps me sleep well. I go to sleep with a satisfied mind and heart, with no worries.'

Sathya Sriram has a sleep preparation routine that includes listening to a short meditation on the Headspace app and soaking her feet in Epsom salts.

Binu Jacob, chairman and CEO of Nestlé for Vietnam, says, 'I sleep by 9.30 p.m. and wake up by 5.30 a.m. I need my eight hours of sleep every day. I try and plan my other commitments around this.'

We have so far explored the three key aspects of physical well-being: physical exercise, nutrition and hydration and sleep. Ensuring that we pay adequate importance to all of these can help us stay physically fit and active, and this in turn can lead to overall well-being.

Kaplesh Parmar effectively incorporates all these three elements into his daily life. He says, 'I start the weekday with exercise [a mix of weight training, walking, badminton, cycling and golf]. I ensure I get good quality and quantity of sleep by sleeping on time and waking up early, and I am particular about having good nutritious food and staying hydrated. I also share health tips with my teams so that they can stay healthy as well.'

So does **Melda Yasar Cebe, ex-MD of The Kraft Heinz Company**. She says, 'I eat healthy; I don't have any junk food; I prefer home-cooked food. I ensure that I get my eight hours of sleep. I enjoy my walk. I try to do 10,000 steps a day. Walking is like meditation. I also sometimes use my walk time to take calls or listen to podcasts.'

What then stops us from doing this on a regular basis? The reasons vary from 'I am fine, I don't think I need this' and 'I will start tomorrow' to 'I don't have the time'. They may all seem like valid reasons, but as we have seen, the benefits of physical well-being are foundational to our ability to be able to perform to our potential. Leaders would do well to find ways of overcoming these barriers by weaving in the aspects of physical well-being into their daily routines. It's great if you already have a regular fitness routine; please make sure to keep at it. In case you don't, please find one at the earliest and then devise a plan to turn it into a habit.

In his book *Atomic Habits*,[31] James Clear talks about the four laws of Cue-Craving-Response-Reward as a basis for building good habits and getting rid of bad habits. He says that to build good habits, you need to make it obvious [cue], make it attractive [craving], make it easy [response] and make it satisfying [reward].

One tip for building good habits is setting an implementation intention—making a specific plan on when and where, having a buddy or a community to work with and habit stacking along with other established good habits.

Let's say that you pick 'going for a walk/run every evening' as a physical activity that you would like. You could try habit stacking—stack the new habit that you want to create along with an existing habit. You could tell yourself that when you take off your work clothes once you return home from work, you will change into your workout clothes and go for a walk or a run. These hacks, when practised over a period of two to three weeks, will help establish the new routine as an ongoing habit.

Many people may be reluctant to exercise or even go for a walk out of laziness or busyness. Temptation bundling works by combining something you enjoy and look forward to with a not-so-enjoyable activity. **Pramath Sinha** loves listening to Hindustani classical music and combines this with regular walking as a form of temptation bundling.

Nirupama likes to walk with a friend and looks forward to social interaction as an aspect of the walking routine. She also uses this time to call family or a friend from a different city as an attractive part of the evening walk.

Toshan Tamhane sums up the importance of physical well-being by saying, 'If you don't find time for health, you will find time for sickness.'

In 2025, we (Rajesh and Nirupama) attended an Ayurvedic Program, which helped us to understand the body and become more mindful about gut health and overall wellness. We plan to continue this and make it an annual practice to refresh and rejuvenate ourselves.

Practical tips for physical well-being

1. **Make physical exercise part of your daily routine:** Weave physical activity into your daily schedule.

Find a swatch of time at work when you can go for a walk; take the stairs instead of the elevator; go on 'walking meetings' with your colleagues and always travel with your walking shoes.
2. **Leverage habit stacking and temptation bundling:** Build new habits by stacking them against an existing habit. Combine something that you enjoy and look forward to with some physical activity that you may not enjoy so much [watching Netflix while cycling in the gym].
3. **Maintain a physical well-being tracker:** What gets tracked gets done; keep a daily tracker that can serve both as a reminder of your progress and the need to stay the course. Share it with a buddy and motivate each other. Use a wearable tracker to track key health indicators.
4. **Prepare well to sleep well:** Establish a realistic bedtime and stick to it every night, if possible even on the weekends. Consider a 'screen ban' on televisions, computers, tablets, cell phones and other electronic devices in the bedroom; instead, read a book before going to bed. Abstain from caffeine, alcohol and large meals in the hours leading up to bedtime.
5. **Consume mindfully:** Each body and each digestive system is different. Everyone has a different relationship with food. If there are issues with the fitness and nutrition levels, it is better to invest in getting customized nutrition advice for your body instead of following fad diets. Eat what is right for you and hydrate well.
6. **Build a well-being culture:** Lead from the front and work towards building a culture of fitness in the organization. A fit, healthy and happy organization

will be an energizing, happy and more productive place to work in.

NOURISH YOUR BODY

- PHYSICAL EXERCISE

 • HABIT STACKING

- MAINTAIN A TRACKER

 • SLEEP WELL

- HYDRATE WELL

 • BUILD A WELL-BEING CULTURE

5

Sharpen Your Mind

'Give me six hours to chop down a tree and I will spend the first four sharpening the axe.'

—Abraham Lincoln

The domain of the mind relates to the focus and sharpness of our energy. We often use the word mental health to denote the state of our mind. While mental health relates to our emotional, psychological and social well-being, mental energy is about stimulating and keeping the mind agile, able and alert.

In today's hyperconnected world, which has a plethora of distractions combined with an overload of information, the mind can feel scattered and confused. Leaders, especially CEOs, need to make decisions quickly and correctly. One of the most common challenges that CEOs face is rapid, unprecedented change. What was right and true yesterday will not be so next week. Leaders need to keep pace, unlearn and learn again; this requires mental agility.

CEOs have multiple distractions and demands on their time and mind. They do not have the luxury of deep immersion in a particular problem. They have to be at peak performance all the time while dealing with numerous issues and a whole variety of tasks. They have to balance the bigger vision with operational details. They are constantly balancing paradoxes and reconciling dilemmas.

Tony Schwartz and Catherine McCarthy connect the mental domain to the focus of energy.[32] According to them, many executives view multitasking as a necessity in the face of all the demands they juggle, but it actually undermines productivity. Distractions are costly. A temporary shift in attention from one task to another—for instance, stopping to answer an e-mail or take a phone call—increases the amount of time necessary to finish the primary task by as much as 25 per cent, a phenomenon known as 'switching time.'

Many leaders have been intentional in making time to recharge mentally. Bill Gates goes off the grid into a cabin at Hood Canal in Washington for a Think Week. He stays there alone, just reading, writing and thinking for seven days. He compares the brain to the CPU of a computer.

In Bill's words:

> You write down all these things . . . then you think, okay do I need to read some books about this? Who do I need to talk to about that? And some things, I say to myself, 'Hey, I just need to think.' It's CPU time. When you write down these things to think about, that's like the code.[33]

Other leaders have their own ways of cutting down on distractions, staying focused and productive.

Jeff Bezos, the CEO of Amazon, has a 'two pizza rule' for meetings. Never have a meeting in which two pizzas couldn't feed all the people present. In this way, only the people who really need to be present to contribute to a meeting are actually there. It is also a way to stick to the essentials of a meeting, a conversation or a task to be accomplished.

Yet Bezos also allows certain meetings to run over time to allow for creative engagement and idea generation. This free-flowing bouncing of ideas in a room of smart people who are trying to solve a problem is stimulating and enjoyable.

The psychologist Mihaly Csikszentmihalyi described a state called 'Flow'. He says, 'The best moments in our lives are not the passive, receptive, relaxing times ... The best moments usually occur if a person's body or mind is stretched to its limits in a voluntary effort to accomplish something difficult and worthwhile.'[34]

The vast amount of research built into this work has explored how the brain changes when entering a flow state in a way that minimizes distraction, maximizes productivity and performance, and eliminates procrastination.

Getting into this Flow state requires us to be fully present, focused, mindful, skilled and balanced. To do this, we need to nurture the mental domain.

We can nurture the mental domain through **heightened focus, continuous learning** and **intellectual engagement**. The leaders we spoke to adopt a variety of ways to nurture the mental domain.

Heightened focus: Mindfulness, minimizing distractions and physical activity

Are we sometimes being mindful, or is our mind always full?

The mind is an amazing tool for decision-making and problem-solving, but it's not very good at being quiet. The core job of the mind is to think, analyse and figure things out. Left to its own devices, the mind will constantly seek out new stimuli, new things to think about and new ways to check out from reality.

Most of the time, the mind is either thinking of the past or dreaming about the future. It is rarely in the present.

What this means is that the mind is full of thoughts, stories and narratives that don't necessarily have anything to do with what's actually happening at the moment. The mind is forever busy and full. Allowing our minds to remain blank without any thoughts, even if for short periods of time, can help in resetting focus and keeping it fresh.

Here, we will talk about three ways in which this can be done: mindfulness, minimizing social distractions and engaging in physical activities.

Practise Mindfulness

There are many definitions of mindfulness.

Mindfulness is the practice of gently focusing your awareness on the present moment over and over again. It often involves focusing on sensations to root yourself in your body in the here and now.

Mindfulness is a practice to notice what is happening in the present moment, without any judgement.

Mindfulness is the awareness of one's internal states and surroundings.

While the definitions may vary, the core essence of mindfulness is about 'living in the moment'. It is a practice to gently retrain the mind to settle into the present moment.

There are several benefits of mindfulness. The greater awareness that we are able to generate by being mindful can help us make better decisions, work more efficiently and effectively and build stronger relationships. There are studies that show that practising mindfulness on a regular basis can reduce stress and anxiety and enhance an overall sense of well-being.

Mindfulness can be practised in many ways:

- Set aside a time for being with yourself and meditate, even if for a brief period of time.
- Every once in a while, do some mindful breathing wherever you are.
- Go for a mindful walk and observe things around you.
- Journaling in the moment can be a great way to practice mindfulness.

Mansi Tripathy, chairman of Shell India, says, 'Diary writing at the end of the day helps me reflect on my own behaviour. It helps me to catch the areas that cause me stress and understand when my own emotions are not in control. I am able to identify my own triggers, and then when I see them coming, I can handle them. Super hyper self-awareness has been very helpful.'

Sudhir Sitapati has been an ardent practitioner of Vipassana for the last seven years. He was introduced to it by a friend, and there's been no looking back. Sudhir says, 'Vipassana meditation helped me become more aware of myself and my ego. It's given me a lot of mental peace, and I now regularly meditate every week.'

Uttam Digga, founder and CEO of Porter, feels that being fully present is extremely important. 'I don't dwell in the past or think about the future. I disassociate myself from the issue, and this helps to reduce negative energy.' Uttam also has a mindful meditation practice, which he does three to four times a week.

Ratna Vishwanathan, CEO of Teach to Reach, talks about chanting as a means of achieving mental well-being. 'Chanting settles me down; it clears my mind and helps me stay calm. I now take time out to step back and think; it has made me more aware and, at some level, less egoistic. I do forty minutes of chanting in the morning and twenty minutes in the evening.'

Apurva Purohit says, 'I need my me-time every day when I don't want to talk to anyone. I use this time for my reading or knitting—it's meditative.'

Sathya Sriram likes her quiet time. 'I like my quiet time, either reading an article or looking at some of the photos that I have taken in the past. This makes me energized and happy.'

Lt Gen. Anil Kumar Bhatt (retd), director general of the Indian Space Association, started yoga twenty years ago. 'I do yoga and meditation. I focus on the present, pay attention to my breath and still my mind. I practise every morning for one hour—it is my me-time. It has helped me be more calm, collected and clear headed. Small things have stopped bothering me.'

Malika Datt Sadaani, founder of The Moms Co., has discovered a unique way to declutter the mind—by organizing her cupboard. 'I find this therapeutic,' she says. 'As I arrange my clothes and personal items, it brings a sense of order and clarity to my thoughts as well.'

Minimize distractions

Nirupama has to enforce the 'no cell phones' rule during workshops, as it creates a great interference to learning and concentration. She does not look at her phone at all during the session, except during breaks since a new email or text message reduces focus on the present task.

Rajesh tracks screen time actively, and if he feels that he has exceeded the usual quota, he makes an effort to reduce the time on the phone.

It's important to note that one can't experience Flow if distractions disrupt the experience. Thus, to experience this state, one has to stay away from the attention-robbers common in a modern fast-paced life. A first step would be to turn off your smartphone when seeking Flow.

We are constantly bombarded by notifications from various social media platforms, which distract us from the work that we are doing or the conversations that we are having. These distractions have a direct impact on our productivity. It also leads to a hyperactive state of our mind, which can have long-term consequences on our well-being.

Minimizing social media distractions can help in channelizing our energy and focusing on the task at hand. This will help us perform those tasks more efficiently and effectively. Most parents have told their children to stop watching TV, playing games or being on the phone during homework or exam time. As adults, we have no one to parent us. So, we need to become that strict parent and tell ourselves to keep away from distractors. While some time on social media or watching cricket or Netflix is good as a relaxation option, we should not become slaves to it.

Nisaba Godrej says, 'Good digital habits are key; how you plan your phone time is very important. I limit my time on social media. Instead I do the *New York Times* crossword.'

Vivek Gambhir sets aside an hour at night where he does not look at technology. 'I put the phone for charging far away from me so that I don't look at the phone the first thing I get up in the morning. Developing micro habits is important. It is important to make those small changes. There is power in compounding changes.'

Physical activity

There is a strong connection between physical well-being and mental well-being. While we discussed the importance of exercise in the previous chapter, many leaders talk about the connection between physical activities and mental well-being. This can happen in two ways. At one level, physical activity helps in emptying the mind and reaching a 'zen state', allowing a much-deserved rest from external distractions. At another level, it helps maintain singular focus on an issue and find creative solutions.

I, Nirupama, get many of my ideas for my writing while walking. It helps me to tune out and tune in to another frequency.

Alok Mittal, co-founder and CEO of Indifi technologies and Global Board member of TiE, is passionate about running and regularly runs three to four days every week. He says, 'When running, my mind is blank; it helps me replenish my mental energy.' Alok also recently started flying lessons and dreams of getting his pilot certification in the coming months. He says that flying helps him focus and be in the moment.

Sucheta Govil says, 'I run 5 km around five to six times a week; it helps me build physical and mental stamina. It helps my brain to rewire in many different ways and that's when I am able to think at my best.'

Clive Kornitzer practises active mindfulness through exercise, boxing or clay pigeon shooting, as they all require total focus.

Sandeep Kataria finds that indulging in competitive sports like badminton or skiing helps quiet the mind and gives a break from the constant chatter. 'When I am on the slopes or playing a sport, I am fully in the moment. More than the physical aspect, these activities give my thinking mind a rest. I also have simple rituals that help me rest and recharge. I am able to get back to work on Monday with greater focus and clarity.'

Continuous learning: Reading, listening to podcasts, writing, teaching, speaking and learning new skills

Henry Ford once famously said, 'Anyone who stops learning is old, whether at twenty or eighty. Anyone who keeps learning stays young. The greatest thing in life is to keep your mind young.'

Continuous learning is about being curious and having the hunger to learn on an everyday basis. Learning about what is happening around us is a fundamental way to ensure that we are keeping ourselves mentally agile. Many leaders talk about the importance of learning on an ongoing basis to stay relevant.

Rakesh Sharma, executive director of Bajaj Auto, says, 'I am curious by nature, and I am constantly learning through my various encounters with people, especially when I am travelling. I actively seek out conversations with a diverse set of people and learn from them.'

Neuroplasticity of the brain is not limited to youth. The brain can change and adapt through our lives, responding to new stimuli and experiences. Dr Andrew Huberman, a scientist at Stanford University, has shown through his research that the brain can be rewired with focused effort.[35]

New learning and new experiences enable learning and keep the brain active. This involves investing time, effort and energy into learning from various sources. These could include reading, listening to podcasts, writing articles, teaching and public speaking.

Taking intentional breaks to sharpen the axe helps us to be more productive and save time in the long run.

Reading and listening to podcasts.

Reading is critical to our personal and professional growth. Reading books and articles, and in today's context, listening to podcasts can be a great way to ensure our mental well-being and, in the process, become better leaders. Reading as well as listening to podcasts elevates our thinking, enhances our empathy levels, increases our vocabulary and makes us happy. Books and podcasts provide concepts and frameworks that can be applied in our workplace to solve challenges and issues. Leaders get exposed to new ideas and perspectives, which they can then 'lift and shift' to solve challenges in their work context. This keeps their mind fresh and agile.

There is a strong correlation between being an avid reader and a thought leader. Many of the leaders who put forth pathbreaking thoughts and perspectives are avid readers, who are then able to effectively connect the dots between the various things that they read about.

Reading also enhances our emotional well-being; we become more empathetic and able to look at things from the other person's perspective. It ultimately makes us a more holistic and well-rounded person and leader.

Debjani Ghosh says, 'I listen to a lot of podcasts—on technology, economics, politics, etc. I learn from talking to people. I find reading to be extremely stimulating both mentally and emotionally. It helps me learn new things, keep myself updated and also makes me happy.'

Shiv Shivakumar says, 'I am continuously looking ahead at cutting-edge industries and following thought leaders. This helps me pick up best practices and new business models. Leaders need to focus on a few things every day and many things over the year. Focus means having no distractions.'

Aditya Sehgal, ex-COO and president at Reckitt PLC, is an avid reader. 'I read a lot. I am in a different world when I read. I read before sleeping and also whenever I get time during the day. I read 127 books in 2023. Reading helps me stay focused and shuts down the monkey brain. It is a silent state—it is important for the resilience of the brain. Reading makes me creative—I am thinking about the issues that I am dealing with at a subconscious level. I like reading science fiction, fantasy and self-help books.'

Puneet Chandok says, 'I read something every day—I try to finish one book every week. I also set aside thirty minutes every day for learning, especially listening to podcasts.'

One of the arguments that you hear many times against reading is, 'I don't have time. There is so much to do.' Some of the smartest people on the planet actively seek learning by devoting time to reading. Warren Buffett is known to devote five to six hours of reading every day. Mark Zuckerberg publicly took on a goal to read one book every two weeks. Some sources say that Bill Gates reads fifty books in a year. If some of these super successful people can find time to read, I am sure many of us can too.

Rajesh Jejurikar, executive director and CEO (auto and farm sector), Mahindra & Mahindra Ltd, says, 'I am a member of a closely knit book club that meets every six weeks. This keeps me going on the habit of reading, and it also has enabled some close friendships.'

It is important to carve out your reading time and protect it at all costs.

Writing

Writing articles and blogs and sharing their thoughts is a great way for leaders to keep their minds active. Writing helps us to reflect upon what we read, hear or see and then connect the dots across different thoughts and synthesize them into meaningful content that can be of use to others. It also mentally stimulates us and leads to mental well-being.

Many leaders share their thoughts through writing on platforms like LinkedIn, their personal blogs, or in some cases, by writing a book. Some of the leaders we interviewed for this book are authors in their own right. Shiv Shivakumar, Sudhir Sitapati, Narasimhan Eswar, Pramath Sinha and Vivek Gambhir have all published their books over the last few years and also happen to be avid readers.

Public speaking and teaching

Speaking at forums and being part of panel discussions is another great way to ensure mental agility. Almost all of the leaders we interviewed talked about being a part of key forums such as Confederation of Indian Industry (CII), Federation of Indian Chambers of Commerce and Industry (FICCI) and other industry bodies and actively participating in industry symposiums. Preparing for these sessions requires leaders to read up, structure their thoughts and create content that is relevant to the context.

'In learning you will teach, and in teaching you will learn' goes the lyric of a Phil Collins song titled 'Song of Man'. Teaching courses and conducting guest lectures at universities during evenings and weekends is another great way for leaders to stay mentally agile. Teaching requires preparation, which enhances one's learning. Also, interacting with the younger generations opens one's mind to a completely different perspective of a very different generation. This helps leaders to unlearn and relearn and keep themselves updated in order to stay relevant.

Shiv Shivakumar is a sought after speaker who enjoys sharing his ideas at different forums. The preparation for the speaker sessions helps him to research and learn more about a variety of topics.

Naveen Munjal, MD of Hero Electric Vehicles Pvt. Ltd, says, 'Teaching at Master Union and conducting a boot camp on the Future of Mobility have been incredibly enriching experiences for me. There is no better way to stay mentally agile and continuously learn than by teaching others. It sharpens my thinking and deepens my own understanding.'

Harit Nagpal, MD of Tata Play, learns new things in a different way. 'For two days a month, I walk through ten to fifteen villages, meeting and learning from people. I've been doing this for the last twenty-five years. It gives me ideas; I find it rejuvenating.'

Nirupama is invited for several talks and panel discussions on women's leadership and diversity, equity and inclusion (DEI). In 2024, she also gave a TEDx talk on the theme, 'Claim Your Power to Find Your Voice'. These speaking sessions help her to research and craft her ideas for the relevant audience.

For **Rajesh,** writing this book was a great learning experience which came from stimulating conversations as well as research.

Learning new skills

Learning new skills has several benefits. It increases mental focus, provides new challenges, gives a sense of purpose and achievement and enables us to connect with like-minded people. Research shows that learning a new skill or a new language increases the neuroplasticity of the brain, helping it to grow, form new connections and rewire itself. This enhances our cognitive functioning and enhances brain volume, memory and functioning.

Nirupama does one course every year on a new topic or picks up a new skill. In 2022, she tried her hand at golf. While golf did not turn out to be her game, the process of learning something new helped her shed some old beliefs and learn about a game she knew little about. Regularly signing up for online or in-person courses, Nirupama invested in a Gestalt coaching programme at the Esalen Institute campus in California in 2023 and a tarot course in 2024. While the themes are related to her work, learning also keeps her mind agile and stimulated. She is now re-learning French which she had studied several years ago in school.

Rajesh started learning to play golf in 2024, and it has been a fascinating journey so far. It is challenging to learn a new skill that requires mind–body coordination. But it is exciting and helps keep his mind stimulated and enhances his focus. He also attended the intense one-month Advanced Management Programme (AMP) at INSEAD, France, in 2022, during his tenure as MD of Perfetti Van Melle. While it is not easy to take a month off from work, Rajesh believes he has immensely benefited from the personal and professional learning derived from the course.

Amrita Randhawa says, 'I take a week off to learn something new. I pick a new theme every three to four months, and I spend four hours of deep learning a week on that theme.'

Radhika Gupta, MD and CEO of Edelweiss Mutual Fund, says, 'I enjoy writing and listening to Urdu poetry, both of which have really helped me with my mental well-being. I also take on projects outside my core area. I give 10 per cent of my professional time as nourishment time—being on *Shark Tank India* and other personal growth projects.'

Hephzibah Pathak, executive chairperson of Ogilvy India, says, 'I love to learn new things. It keeps me energized and mentally stimulated. On the other hand, I also like to de-clutter, physically and mentally. The act of de-cluttering makes me feel more relaxed, focused and find that sweet spot of calm.'

Intellectual engagement: Coaching and mentoring, attending seminars, participating in forums

What is common to Sergei Brin, Eric Schmidt, Sheryl Sandberg, Sundar Pichai, Steve Jobs, Jack Dorsey and Jeff Bezos? Apart from the fact that they have been extremely successful leaders in the world of technology, they were also coached by Bill Campbell, a football coach and a CEO known as the 'Trillion Dollar' coach.

While we will talk about mentoring and coaching later in the book as a means of nurturing others, these can also help us in nurturing ourselves. Mentoring and reverse mentoring can play a key role in our mental well-being. Mentoring forces us to think of possibilities to help and support our mentees, very often leading to the creation of some new perspectives for the mentor as well.

Susanne Arfelt Rajamand, former CEO of Royal Greenland, says, 'I leverage my mentors and coaches to help me for my mental fuel and energy.' **Amit Syngle** says, 'I have a coach who helps me with mental stimulation.'

Vineeta Singh says, 'I use my mentor and my board members as a sounding board to get advice on things that I am unsure of.' **Vinita Bali, former CEO of Britannia Industries,** says, 'I am on the boards of different organizations, and I engage with various executives, which keeps me learning new things. I look at boards as my perennial learning plan. I have been on the boards of a technology company, IIM

Bangalore and Welham Girl's School, and these helped me learn about nutrition, business and academics.'

Anant Goel, co-founder and ex-CEO, Milkbasket, finds it helpful to discuss with other founders and entrepreneurs and learn how they resolve dilemmas. 'This helps me get different perspectives from different people in similar situations,' he says.

Raghu Krishnan, area vice president at Kenvue, says, 'As I have grown into senior leadership roles, I've learnt that no single mentor has all the answers. I work with different coaches—one for hard skills, another for soft skills—and seek out trusted mentors and friends based on their strengths, whether it's culture, strategy, operations or organizational design. This diversity of input helps me lead more effectively.'

Reverse mentoring is increasingly gaining popularity, with leaders leveraging younger generations in the workplace and outside to gain fresh perspectives, especially in the areas of technology, AI and the like. **Amit Jain** talks about reverse mentoring as a means of staying mentally agile and learning what's going on in today's world. Reverse mentoring can help bridge intergenerational gaps and forge strong bonds across layers in the organization. This would not only benefit the concerned individuals but also the organization at large. He says, 'I usually have a young mentor at any point in time who helps me stay updated on the happenings in today's world. It keeps me young.'

Anusha Shetty loves to spend time with her younger Gen Z employees because she learns a lot about the digital world and technology from them.

Kirthiga Reddy, CEO of Verix and ex-MD of Meta India, strongly believes in getting a coach for different aspects of her life. 'I used to have an executive coach most of my life; I wish

I had started earlier. I have an extensive set of coaches—career coach, life coach, therapist—to enhance my performance.'

Hitesh Oberoi, co-promoter, MD and CEO of Infoedge India Ltd, says, 'I like to be in touch with what's happening around me, I need to keep learning and updating myself. I learn from start-ups, new hires in new emerging areas and now even the right handles on Twitter.' **Debjani** goes on to say, 'I consciously do reverse mentoring with the young crowd. I learn a lot from them, especially about technology. I do "Lunch with the Bunch" to learn about new things.'

Attending seminars and engaging with thought leaders further stimulates intellectual engagement. Many leaders are intentional about attending select conferences, which helps them to widen their worldview, learn from experts and engage with a diverse group of people.

The AMP course that Rajesh attended in France not only enhanced learning but also enabled connections with senior leaders from different cultures and industries. This opened up his mind, and the conversations outside the classroom were just as stimulating as the discussions inside.

So far we have seen how continuous learning, intellectual engagement and heightened focus can help in our mental energy management. Practising some of these on an ongoing basis keeps our mind fresh and agile.

Practical tips for nurturing the mental domain

1. **Set aside learning time:** Nurturing the mental domain requires discipline and dedication. Keep some time aside every day/week for learning. Set goals that work for you, such as reading ten pages every day or finishing one book a month. Solving

crossword puzzles, Wordle or Sudoku daily also helps keep the mind sharp and agile.
2. **Get a coach and a mentor:** Coaching and mentors can broaden your perspective. Investing in a professional coach is critical for learning and growth. Look for a leader you admire, whose career path and values inspire you. Approach that person to be your mentor.
3. **Minimize distractions—be your own parent:** Consciously minimize screen time and time spent on social media. Use that more productively. Practise mindfulness on a regular basis.
4. **Surround yourself with people who are smart:** Confident leaders hire smart people. Hire smart and stay humble so that you can learn from them. This will take care of both learning and intellectual engagement. Join a peer group of like-minded people who can provide intellectual stimulation.
6. **Enhance and share your knowledge:** Pick a learning course that is relevant for you. After attending that, share the knowledge with your team. Write an article on LinkedIn summarizing your learnings. Putting yourself out there to speak at forums will make you research the topics and also expose you to other points of view.

SHARPEN YOUR MIND

- SET ASIDE LEARNING TIME

- GET A MENTOR/COACH

- MINIMIZE DISTRACTIONS

- SURROUND YOURSELF WITH SMART PEOPLE

- ENHANCE & SHARE YOUR KNOWLEDGE

6

Open Your Heart

'The less you open your heart to others, the more your heart suffers.'
—Deepak Chopra

Have you had a day when you may not have physically left your office but felt exhausted and drained at the end of the day?

We all have.

It is difficult to sustain positive emotions throughout the day. We all have situations and stressors that can lead to negative emotions that take a toll on us. Very often, there is emotional fatigue.

Giving feedback to team members.
Receiving feedback from board members.
Managing a crisis at work.
Managing a crisis at home.
Dealing with the pressure of meeting targets.
Dealing with the pressure of attrition.

This list is endless. Many CEOs believe that a lot of their time is spent putting out business fires and emotional outbursts.

Leaders are tasked with the responsibility of managing other people's emotions. They are cultural custodians who need to keep up the spirit and spread positive energy. They cannot do this if they are unable to manage their own emotions and nourish the emotional domain. Opening your heart is about being open to expressing and receiving emotions. While the limbic brain is associated with emotional control, the heart is the common metaphor for any kind of deep feeling.

Leaders need to tune in to the emotions of others and be perceptive and empathetic towards the needs of several other people. To do this, they need to first manage their own emotions.

Emotional intelligence and its importance

The concept of emotional intelligence is not new. This is a critical capability for leaders. In 2003, the *Harvard Business Review*[36] reported that 80 per cent of the competencies that differentiate top performers from others are emotional intelligence competencies. Daniel Goleman, the author of *Emotional Intelligence*, defined this as the ability to be aware of and manage your emotions and the ability to be aware of and manage others' emotions.

There are four aspects of emotional intelligence: self-awareness, self-regulation, social awareness and relationship management.

Self-awareness is the first step.

This is not easy.

Nirupama starts many workshops through a check-in process. Leaders are asked to answer the question, 'How are you feeling?'

Most people say 'good', 'fine' or 'okay'. They cannot describe how they are really feeling.

We rarely talk about how we are really feeling. For a long time, the world of emotions has not been associated with the world of work. We have admired stoicism, grit, resilience and the ability to manage and overcome emotions rather than use them and accept them.

Naming our emotions is the first step in understanding and managing them. This helps in our emotional well-being and mental health.

The next stage is to regulate the expression of emotions. This is more challenging. The pressure and stress in the workplace create many moments of tension.

All the leaders we interviewed admitted that there were moments when they felt stressed, frustrated, irritated and fearful. They have built coping mechanisms to deal with them because an inability to handle these triggered reactions can have a long-lasting negative consequence.

We get triggered when we feel threatened or fearful even though there might not be a real threat to our physical well-being. The brain immediately releases adrenaline and cortisol to manage the stress.

One of the leaders coached by Nirupama reported that he would get angry when a team member's deliverable would not meet expectations. He would raise his voice, use harsh words and say things that he would regret later. He tried to control his temper but was not able to do so. During the coaching sessions, he was able to identify his own fear of failure as the trigger for these outbursts. When a team member did not perform, he saw it as his own failure. He was worried about how his boss would react to him. This caused the immediate reaction.

Our brain goes into a fight, flight or freeze mode when confronted with these triggers. This is a part of evolutionary biology to keep us safe from dangers. While these reactions create an adrenaline rush that helps us to run from a wild animal or fight back, they do not help in interpersonal relationships.

Therefore, it is important for leaders to nurture themselves emotionally to be able to handle the daily emotional roller coaster ride that their job entails. They need to find creative ways to put back what the role can sometimes take from them.

Wise leaders realize this and are intentional about finding ways to keep refuelling their emotional energy. In our conversations with the leaders, we found three distinct ways in which they nurture and manage the emotional domain.

Positive outlook

Our mindset matters. Our emotional state is governed to a large extent by our fundamental philosophy of life.

Martin Seligman, a psychologist known as the pioneer in the field of positive psychology, described two ways of looking at life. In his book *Learned Optimism*,[37] he described the Optimistic Approach and the Pessimistic Approach. His studies found a strong correlation between an optimistic attitude and the mental and emotional health of the person. The explanatory style we use when we face setbacks and failures has an impact on our emotions. Do we blame ourselves, feel victimized or do we take responsibility and move forward?

Positive thinking helps to reduce stress and negative emotions. People with a positive outlook are better at finding solutions and support. Many of the leaders we spoke to shared their outlook, which enables them to stay emotionally healthy, stable and recover quickly from setbacks.

Ratna Vishwanathan says, 'I am pathologically optimistic.' This has helped her to weather challenges in her personal and professional life. **Ayushi Gudwani, founder**

and CEO of FS Life, also credits her genuine optimistic mindset for her emotional resilience. She says, 'When I have bad days and feel low, I ask myself the question, Do I want to switch roles with anyone else in the world? The answer is always no. This helps me stay happy in my own context.'

'I try not to take anything too seriously. Life is just a gig and so is work. I took a break when I turned forty and learnt the tabla for a year. I live for the moment by creating micro-moments of having fun,' says **C.V.L. Srinivas, country manager, WPP India.**

Harsh Mariwala says, 'I follow a simple life philosophy—be happy and add value to others. Live simply without negativity.' **Geetika Mehta** says, 'I think of life as a marathon and not a sprint. It keeps me in a learn and unlearn mode and helps me to stay grounded.'

'Don't get caught up with the regrets of the past,' says **Aditya Ghosh.** 'Today is the best time of my life. It helps me to have emotional equilibrium.' **Bharat Puri, MD of Pidilite,** provides an interesting perspective on emotional well-being. He says, 'I am an eternal optimist. I always see something positive in any situation. I look at things from a distance and don't get too carried away by the situation.'

Harit Nagpal says, 'I don't let the bucket empty out so that there is a need to fill it up; I avoid exhaustion, and I don't worry too much about things. I operate as a consultant for my business—I detach myself from the business—it reduces my depletion.'

Ashish Dhawan, founder and CEO of the Convergence Foundation, believes in the philosophy of attached detachment. He knows that everything is not within his control. The idea of *nishkam karm* [meaning 'selfless action' or 'action without desire'] keeps him grounded. 'Happiness is reality minus expectations. I have learnt to reset expectations through mental tuning.'

Navneet Saluja, Area GM of Haleon, says, 'I am very comfortable in my skin. I am not harsh on myself and make sure that I have fun and enjoy life.' **Saugata Gupta of Marico** echoes the sentiment. He says, 'Don't take yourself too seriously. It will create more stress. Be humble; chill in life. Make sure you take those breaks and don't carry work pressures home.'

'Fear, competition and comparison are three things that limit our potential and well-being,' says **Ramesh Mangaleswaran, Senior Partner Emeritus, McKinsey & Company**. Letting go of these can bring us greater equanimity and also take us to the next level of growth. 'I focus on what I can control,' shares **Sunil D'souza of Tata Consumer Products**. He echoes the model of 'Circle of Influence' and 'Circle of Concern'. 'I keep moving forward. Doing something and making some progress is better than doing nothing. Momentum counts for something.'

Strong connections

Strong, nurturing connections also help energize us emotionally. Whether the leader identifies as an introvert who gets energy from within or as an extrovert who gets energy from outside, strong connections help in emotional nourishment. We have seen that while some leaders have a very active social life and draw energy from multiple connections and activities, others get emotional energy from a few deep connections, especially from their immediate family.

While some are very intentional about initiating and sustaining connections, other leaders have an organic approach to nurturing relationships. All leaders believe that emotional anchors and a supportive network not only at the workplace but also outside are important to maintain an emotional balance.

Our inner circle is a close group of friends or family who offer us a safe space to talk, cry, share and discharge our emotions. Leaders may not be able to do this easily with colleagues at work; therefore, the inner circle connections are important. Often, we take these people for granted, especially if they are close family members. Sometimes, we do not make time to cultivate and invest in our inner circle. Relationships flourish when they are nurtured.

Some people may have a wide circle. For others, two or three people may be enough. But create and hold on to these connections since they are your emotional harbour. Appreciate these members. Remember important occasions in their lives. Be there for them when they need you. Ask for help when you need it.

Join a community of like-minded people who can become your inner circle. Organizations like Young Presidents' Organization (YPO), Entrepreneurs' Organization (EO) and Offline provide small group connections that can grow to become your trusted inner circle. Or you could develop them with people who share a common passion. 'I have very warm connections. I have a personal board of directors. These are people with whom I have a safe space to discuss anything,' says **Greet Boonen, CEO of RainPharma Belgium.**

Anand Kripalu, MD of EPL says, 'I usually have a happy temperament. I get a lot of energy from our social group. We have a great group of ex-Unilever folks; we holiday together and are there for each other.'

'Since my travel schedule is hectic, my real downtime comes from being with my family. This relaxes me,' says **Sameer Suneja, group CEO of Perfetti Van Melle.**

'I have an active social life and make it a point to meet people over the weekend, whether it is during golf or after,' says **Varun Berry**. Connection with pets can also be energising. **Ram Raghavan** says 'I get to experience unconditional love from my dog. It reduces my stress levels.'

Amrita Randhawa loves cooking for others over the weekend. It is her way of showing love and affection. Time spent with her daughter is a big source of emotional nourishment for her.

Toshan Tamhane believes that time for connection also needs to be scheduled and planned. He intentionally sets Sunday aside for family time and ensures that the family eats dinner together at home. He plans one trip or activity with a family member over the weekend.

Being intentional also works for **Neil George**. He makes it a point to call his friends on their birthday. It is mandatory for the family to spend Saturday afternoons at the dining table, from 10 a.m. to 2 p.m. and have Sunday breakfast together as a family post their Church mass. He and his wife also have a Friday date night ritual, given the rigorous travel schedule that takes him away from his place of residence during the week. **Radhika Gupta** draws a lot of emotional energy from her one-year-old son. She keeps all her spare time to be with him, play with him and take him to different places.

For **Tarun Arora, CEO of Zydus Wellness,** spending time with his two children, aged ten and thirteen, is important. He plays various games, such as chess and table tennis, with them and supports his son's passion for football. This builds connection with his children and also reduces his stress levels.

Achal Agrawal, ex-Kimberly Clark, has frequent coffee catch-ups with different people. He makes himself available to people who request such connections and finds it energizing to listen to them and offer any support.

Vineeta Singh also believes in the value of friendship. 'There is the joy of women friends. I'm part of group of women founders and we have a WhatsApp group chat, which is a non-judgemental space. Sometimes, reconnecting with a childhood friend and having an honest conversation, even crying it out for a bit, can be really cathartic. As a leader, it can get lonely at times, so having a circle where you can truly be yourself without the pressure to always have it together, makes a difference.'

For **Kaushik Mukherjee, co-founder and COO of SUGAR Cosmetics,** the quality of connections also matters. 'I have limited time to spend. So I invest in a few connections and go deep.' **B. Govindarajan, CEO of Royal Enfield,** surrounds himself with people who give him positive energy. Riding his bike, feeling the connection between man, machine and terrain, also helps him relax.

I, **Rajesh**, have an extensive social network and intentionally keep time apart for connecting with others. I make it a point to call people to wish them on birthdays and meet friends while travelling to their cities. When I had taken a break from work, I would connect with at least one person everyday for a coffee catch up. These connections greatly energise me and I find it very fulfilling to engage with different types of people.

Passions and other interests

The workaholic CEO who has no life outside the office is no longer a tenable archetype. It is important to find something else that gives you joy, satisfaction and makes for a holistic life. Go back to a childhood passion—something you enjoyed in your youth and that has given you happy memories.

For me, **Rajesh,** photography is more than a hobby. It is a passion that not only energizes me but also helps me in my work. I feel that photography drew me out of my comfort zone and helped me connect with strangers easily. Photography also helps me focus better, gain new perspectives and make me a better leader.

Nirupama loves writing. She started with short articles, humorous pieces for the *Economic Times*, short stories for magazines and eventually two novels: *Keep the Change* (2010) and *Intermission* (2012). She now wants to go back to her childhood hobby of sketching and painting.

While a passion or hobby need not become a second career, it helps to have some other safe and happy space to go to. 'It is important to have a host of interests outside of work,' says **Suparna Mitra, CEO of Titan.** She goes on to add, 'There is a time to be fallow and a time to be fertile. You can't be harvesting forever.' **Yamini Bhat, co-founder and CEO of Vymo,** says, 'Painting is my form of meditation, and I paint at least once every weekend.'

Rahul Shankar is passionate about music. 'I love singing. It is a soul food for me and also acts as a stress buster. I started singing seriously four to five years ago. Recently, a few of us from the corporate world formed a band. We perform at popular clubs in Delhi/NCR. Singing pumps me up and gives me my dopamine. My job requires me to go up on stage regularly and I use these opportunities to sing as well and convey my message through that.'

Narasimhan Eswar, MD of Whirlpool, echoes the sentiment: 'I am passionate about music. I can get lost in music and go into a different zone. I love diverse kinds of music, and the language really doesn't matter. I feel very happy when I'm listening to music.' **Alpana Titus,** who enjoys photography and gardening, says, 'Downtime is very important to rebuild your personal energy.'

Naveen Munjal says, 'I am passionate about photography, especially street photography, which I find both therapeutic and meditative. It is a great stress buster and has led to many energizing and unexpected connections. When combined with travel, the experience becomes deeply liberating. My passion was reignited in 2013 during a workshop with Jay Maisel in New York. I shoot, I capture, I smile and sometimes I am moved by the depth of emotion that a single image can hold.'

Vikas Chawla is also energized by nature and combines his passion for travelling with time spent in nature.

Nisaba Godrej loves horse riding. This is an activity that makes her feel joyful and also calms her. **Vinita Bali, former CEO of Britannia Industries and board member,** has a deep appreciation for the performing arts. She loves listening to music and going to plays, reading and listening to poetry. Doing these activities with her friends helps her to unwind and relax. 'Freestyle dancing is my stressbuster,' says **Neetu Kashiramka, managing director of VIP Industries.** She also loves trying out new recipes from YouTube and cooks one dish every weekend.

Susanne Artfelt Rajamand is always looking to replenish her energy bank. 'Horse riding is a passion, but I don't get to do as much of it as I would like to. It gives me peace of mind. I enjoy travelling. I prioritize my holidays; I enjoy being in the mountains, going diving. This gives me a store of energy that I can bank for later.'

Being in touch with nature can be a wonderful passion that has several benefits. Scientists are beginning to find evidence that being in nature has a profound impact on our brains and our behaviour, helping us to reduce anxiety, brooding and stress, and increase our attention capacity, creativity and ability to connect with other people.

Practices like forest bathing, which is popular in Japan, have proven benefits on mental and emotional well-being. Grounding, or earthing, the practice of walking barefoot on grass or submerging yourself fully in nature in different ways, had both physical and emotional healing benefits.

Research at Stanford University showed that those who walked in nature compared to people who walked in urban settings showed different results. Those who walked in nature experienced less anxiety, rumination (focused attention on negative aspects of oneself) and negative affect, as well as more positive emotions, in comparison to the urban walkers.[38]

Mahesh Madhavan, global CEO of Bacardi, is an avid gardener. He says, 'Gardening allows me to stay grounded and connect with Mother Nature; this enables me to disengage with the business. If I weren't doing this job, I would have been a farmer. I grow my own vegetables. It gives me immense fulfilment and satisfaction—I can see the result of my hard work. When I am in the garden, I can spend hours together. I spend about five to six hours on the weekend. We have our own beehive and collect our own honey. It is very therapeutic.'

Managing our emotional energies cannot be left to chance. While all emotions have a gift and come with a message, our inability to manage and regulate our emotional energies will lead to unhealthy situations and dysfunctional relationships.

The 2024 State of Workplace Empathy report from Businessolver[39] showed that 55 per cent of CEOs reported some mental health issues in the past year. At 60 per cent, Millennial CEOs are most likely to have experienced a mental health issue through anxiety, depression, loneliness, obsessive-compulsive disorder or burnout.

A CEO being unable to cope with stress, regulate emotions and make the best decisions has huge ramifications. Unfortunately, many people see mental health issues as a sign of weakness or inability to cope with the pressures of the job. We are ready to get professional help for a host of things—to fix our cars and appliances, to mend our clothes and even to elevate our physical fitness or improve a game. In the same way, it is important to get the help we need to improve our emotional well-being. This will have long-term benefits for us.

Practical tips for nurturing the emotional domain

1. **Create and cultivate an inner circle:** Invest in building connections. Have a close group with whom you can freely share anything. Be part of communities of like-minded people. Talk and share openly in this group.
2. **Find/pursue your passion:** Have a passion or a set of passions outside of work that energize you. Learn something you have always wanted to try but kept putting off because you didn't have the time. Make this a priority rather than a time filler.
3. **Visualize positive outcomes:** Have a growth mindset. Visualize positive outcomes before key meetings. Set a positive intention to manifest a positive reality. Build resilience that helps deal with the not-so-desirable outcomes.
4. **Be close to nature:** Spend time with nature as much as possible. Make the time to go out to a park or garden. Take a break with your inner circle in the mountains or by the sea. Balance online time with offline time, at least by gazing at potted plants or

greenery nearby. Enjoy the emotional calm and release that it brings.

5. **Seek professional help:** Don't shy away from asking for help to maintain emotional well-being. Therapy, life coaching or joining a self-help community are all different ways in which you can seek help. It is important to recognize the early warning signs of depleting emotional energy and take the required help to address it.

OPEN YOUR HEART

- CREATE & CULTIVATE AN INNER CIRCLE
- FOLLOW YOUR PASSION
- VISUALIZE POSITIVE OUTCOMES
- BE CLOSE TO NATURE
- SEEK PROFESSIONAL HELP

7

Enrich Your Soul

'Ask yourself what makes you come alive and then go do that.'

—Howard Thurman

A story that Nirupama heard long ago left a deep impression on her. She often uses it while conducting leadership workshops.

A man came across three stonecutters and asked them what they were doing. The first replied, 'I am making a living.' The second continued hammering as he said, 'I am doing what my boss tells me to do.' The third looked up smiling with a visionary gleam in his eye and said, 'I am building a hospital where the poor people from my village can come to get better.'

All three of them are doing the same work and have legitimate explanations for why they are doing it. But which stonecutter do you think would derive the greatest satisfaction and display a long-term commitment? Which stonecutter has the potential to be the leader of stonecutters?

Leadership is more than making a living or doing a good job. It requires a certain kind of energy that comes from within, an energy that enables the leader to persevere through tough times, contribute to the greater good and take people along.

This is the energy that comes from the soul—the spiritual domain. Soul and spirit are not in a different realm from what we do on a daily basis. Soul is about our inner core, the essence of our dreams, will, imagination, desires and actions. Spirit is about the collective source of energy in the universe that taps into something greater than just the individual. Some of the leaders we spoke to said that they were not religious, but all of them had some connection to the spiritual domain.

Leadership today has evolved from the managerial 'Get things done' model prevalent at the start of the Industrial Revolution to something more nuanced, meaningful and uplifting.

Author of *Leadership With Soul*, former CEO of Burger King and Euro Disney and current CEO of Intertek, Andre Lacroix talks about the importance of this aspect for the modern corporation.[40] He says that while companies are better managed today than even twenty years ago, they are still overmanaged and under led. Good leadership is about inspiring the organization towards a meaningful approach to take the business from point A to point B. It is not enough to get energy only from increasing profitability or growth. Leaders need to get energy from leading people and seeing the organization grow under their leadership.

Corporate leaders today speak about the importance of meaning, purpose, mindfulness and consciousness. It is not just anecdotes about Steve Jobs coming to India to learn meditation and find a guru that indicate this movement, but many leaders speak openly about understanding the self, the importance of enhanced awareness and self-realization.

Meditation is not only a practice for greater mental clarity and acuity but also a way to access the inner core.

American media personality Oprah Winfrey, former CEO of LinkedIn Jeff Weiner, Salesforce head Marc Benioff and Bridgewater Associates chief investment officer Ray Dalio have all spoken in public about the importance of spiritual practices, downtime and deep reflection.

An inner life or spiritual practice is important in the process of enabling personal spiritual leadership and facilitating work that is meaningful and takes place in the context of a community. Many companies are beginning to recognize the importance of supporting an employee's inner life. Cordon Bleu - Tomasso Corporation has established a room for inner silence.[41] Australia and New Zealand Banking Group Ltd (ANZ) have developed training programmes focusing on 'high performance' mind techniques and 'quiet rooms' for individual spiritual practice. Faith-based healthcare organization Ascension, Missouri, is committed to a workplace that deepens personal spirituality through the adoption of an ethical discernment process that fosters self-reflection. These organizations and many others recognize that employees have spiritual needs (i.e., an inner life) just as they have physical, mental and emotional needs, and none of these needs are left at the door when they arrive at work.

Professor Hitendra Wadhwa of Columbia Business School and author of *Inner Mastery, Outer Impact*, has conducted research through his consulting firm Mentora Institute on over 1000 leadership moments where leaders displayed exemplary leadership.[42] In his 2023 *Harvard Business Review* article, 'Leading in the Flow of Work',[43] he states that this was possible by tapping into their inner core—the space of highest potential within them. People have engaged in contemplative practices in an effort to connect with what they have intuited to be their spirit or soul and to express these qualities in outer pursuit.

Even as we nurture the physical, mental and emotional domains, we need to connect deeply to the spiritual domain to sustain the actions we take in the others. Without this aspect, anything we do will be inconsistent, inappropriate and inadequate. When we spoke to leaders, we were able to identify three aspects of the spiritual domain. While some leaders intentionally nurtured this aspect, others felt that it was the solid foundation that impacted all aspects of their lives.

Values and purpose

Nirupama conducts several workshops with leaders to help them identify their purpose. Many leaders have a general sense of purpose but are not able to articulate it well. Successful leaders not only have a clear purpose but also help others identify and articulate that so that they can live up to their highest potential.

Purpose is a desire to serve and contribute to something larger than yourself. It is bigger than goals; goals are milestones on the road to living your purpose. Purpose is bigger than satisfying needs and wants. Having a purpose is bigger than making a New Year's resolution. Though several people may be doing the same job, like the stonecutters, the ones with a sense of purpose can do more and be more. Usually, they become leaders.

Hina Nagarajan says, 'When people identify their purpose, both personally and professionally, and then use work as a platform to shape their legacies, they are sure to succeed. This is the success mantra that I try to inculcate in each of my team members. I believe success is not just about achieving milestones for yourself, but it is about how these are achieved and how many people you take along with you on the journey. I can put my hand on my heart and say that I have worked hard to help my team members discover their purpose and achieve their legacies no matter which company I have been in, and this has created a win-win for the company, me and the communities we have operated within.'

The purpose can be articulated through a personal mission statement or a purpose statement. This is the big 'why' at the heart of the golden circle that author and leadership expert Simon Sinek refers to. A clear sense of purpose provides the energy and fuel to keep going on the lonely, often dangerous path of leadership at scale.

Unilever runs a workshop on purpose, and it is a core driver of its leadership model.[44] Being more purposeful is another way Unilever hopes to attract and retain staff. The brand found almost half (49 per cent) of staff that attended purpose training reported 'higher intrinsic motivation' and resulted in a 25 per cent bump in declarations of being able to 'go the extra mile in their job'.

Arundhati Bhattacharya, CEO and chairperson, Salesforce India and South Asia, believes that spiritual growth is very important for a leader. She says, 'Spirituality is about balance and equanimity; it's about our ability to handle different situations in a balanced manner. Spirituality is also about having a purpose—my purpose is to help others achieve their dreams.'

Binu Jacob says, 'I spent a lot of time discovering what my purpose in life was. I finally distilled it down to the following: to inspire and be inspired to make a meaningful impact at scale. This grounds me and gives me a sense of direction on a daily basis.'

Purpose can also relate to living a life aligned to values. Mahatma Gandhi's mission was to live his values of truth and non-violence. Independence for India was a goal achieved by living these values. Values are universally desirable principles. All values seem important, but some are more core to us than others in the value priority list. Understanding and articulating these values also helps to live a life of purpose. Values provide direction, help us to make decisions when there are conflicting issues and provide a foundation for our unique brand of leadership.

Rajesh worked with a coach a few years ago on articulating his purpose. His purpose is 'to positively inspire and impact people around me and to actively seek new experiences to become a more holistic person.' He says, 'I am blessed to be able to live this on a daily basis through my work, coaching, consulting, photography and travel, and our initiative My Daughter Is Precious.'

Nirupama's purpose is to joyfully live her full potential to lead a powerful life and enable others to do the same. She does this through the work of coaching, facilitation, writing and seeking joy in the little things in life. This helps her conduct multiple workshops for eight to nine hours with energy and enthusiasm since the work directly relates to her purpose and gives her joy.

Mansi Tripathy believes that it is her responsibility to see that the people in the organization are fulfilled about their lives and careers. She brings this to her work through conversations. 'We keep purpose as the central theme for our conversations instead; we make it live and relevant for their job. Helping them see that their work is important and has an impact. Doing it in a systematic manner and talking about it all the time is important.'

Understanding and living by values and purpose becomes even more important during crises. **Suresh**

Narayanan believes that more than half the effort in managing a crisis is to manage yourself. Leaders crumble because of the disconnect between personal strengths, their innate competence and the task at hand. Managing the self and understanding the interplay between purpose, values, emotions and outcomes is a big challenge.

Pankaj Saran, ex-Deputy National Security Advisor (NSA) of India, says, 'I should leave behind a legacy where I have contributed and added value. I should have made a difference in my job. I like to empower those who work for me, to train them, instil confidence and build a sense of pride in them.'

The late Ratan Tata lived by his values of trust, reputation and compassion. The tributes that poured in after his death highlighted how he lived his values, and these were reflected in his leadership style and the organizations that he led.

One of **Rajesh's** core values is connection. This defined his leadership style at Perfetti Van Melle, where he built and maintained excellent relationships across different levels in the organization and outside as well. When connection is a core value, it is easy and natural to focus on relationships rather than just the task. For **Rajeev Dubey, ex-Mahindra & Mahindra**, the three principles of *satya, prem* and *seva* (truth, love and service) act as guiding lights to provide a deep spiritual grounding.

A purpose statement need not always be lofty and noble; it needs to resonate with you and give you energy and excitement. It does include an element of contribution to a cause but need not be confined to it.

Sometimes, it is easy to see a direct connection between your work and a larger purpose that serves humanity. **Pramath Sinha** says that his work in education gives him a strong sense of purpose. Apart from that, he also supports his father's legacy in Hindi literature by building a slew of digital, audio, video and other contemporary formats more relevant to the times. This gives him sustenance.

Ashish Dhawan says, 'India is at a seminal moment in time and has the ability to become a developed nation. My larger purpose for the Convergence Foundation is to create impact at scale and contribute to India's growth and development in that journey. At a personal level, my purpose is to create a positive impact all around me and I am happy when both of these are in total alignment.'

Contribution

Contribution to a cause is an aspect of purpose that can be done directly through the work or outside it. Altruism refers to behaviours that benefit another person or alleviate their distress without any foreseeable extrinsic benefit, and often at a cost, without the expectation of anything in return. Research[45] shows that altruism promotes a sense of well-being and happiness and also leads to health benefits.

While the purpose itself may lead to contribution at scale, active acts of altruism bring a different kind of energy.

Rajesh and Nirupama run a nonprofit initiative called My Daughter Is Precious (MDIP), which provides scholarships and mentorships to young women from underserved backgrounds to complete their college education. They started this work with their daughter Kaavya in 2017 and continue the initiative by taking a cohort of young women through the MDIP programme every year. While this is distinct from their main work, it also feeds into their purpose. Since Nirupama works in the area of gender equality, it is also deeply rooted in her mission to improve the gender balance. It gives a greater sense of contribution and is aligned to her values of connection and contribution. Hearing about the stories of the girls whose lives have been transformed through scholarships and mentorship gives us an immense sense of satisfaction.

Many leaders actively champion corporate social responsibility (CSR) initiatives in their organizations as a way of contributing and derive satisfaction from them, which is different from increasing the bottom line.

Neetu Kashiramka wants to make women more powerful and takes time out for mentoring and supporting women who want to come up in life. This is her way of giving back to society.

Rajesh majorly focused on CSR in his role as MD at Perfetti Van Melle. He says, 'We created the new position of a CSR head, supported the recycling of plastic waste and enabled the education and upliftment of communities near our factories. Watching the happy faces of the schoolchildren we supported and seeing the difference we made during the beautification of a local park gave me a lot of happiness.'

Vikas Chawla believes in 'leadership with heart'. His company supports various causes across the globe with a view towards creating social impact. **Vinita Bali** says, 'I have looked beyond the obvious and connected business to a larger business. When I was in Britannia, we realized that there is a huge deficiency in nutrition in children. It was important for us to address this social issue. In 2007, we fortified our biscuits, like Tiger Biscuits, with micronutrients. We carried out studies and research and got great results. Within every business lies a kernel of being of service to society. We look beyond CSR. We recycle the garbage we generate.'

Mamta Saikia, CEO, Bharti Airtel Foundation, says, 'I am blessed to be able to contribute to the community as part of my work. I gave up a regular corporate job and joined Child Rights and You (CRY) many years ago, and I continue with my desire to contribute even today in my current role at the Bharti Airtel Foundation. Initially, it was a sense of wonder and happiness; now it is a huge sense of responsibility having to take care of so many projects. I sleep every day with the sense of satisfaction and hope for a better future for the kids—it gives me a sense of purpose.'

Deep Kalra has made a conscious decision to devote more time to 'things that matter.' 'I make it a point to meet at least one young entrepreneur each day, engage with the NGOs I support and contribute to institutions such as Ashoka University, IIMA Endowment Fund, CII, WTTC, I Am Gurgaon, etc. Additionally, the work we do at the MakeMyTrip Foundation, especially our sustainability initiatives, fills me with immense joy and pride.'

Radhika Piramal feels that it is important to find a sense of satisfaction outside of work. She does a lot of LGBT advocacy since she has a platform to do this. She gives talks on this subject and helps others by listening and sharing.

Giving to others gives sunshine to the soul. Generosity expands our spirit.

One of the ways of nurturing yourself is to connect to your purpose and values on a regular basis to give yourself the much-needed motivation and energy boost by having a larger positive impact.

Pause for self-reflection

'He who knows others is clever; he who knows himself is enlightened,' said Lao Tzu the Chinese philosopher. Practices that lead to greater self-awareness and reflection help to nurture the spirit. Self-reflection builds self-awareness, and this in turn helps leaders to make the right decisions and move from reaction to response.

Tasha Eurich, author of the book *Insight* has done extensive work on self-awareness.[46] She has found that though 95 per cent of people say that they are self-aware, only 15 per cent of them are actually self-awareness Unicorns, a rare breed of people who are able to see themselves clearly. Those who are self-aware are more fulfilled, less anxious, better communicators and leaders. One of the interesting techniques she describes is the ability to ask the What question instead of the Why questions.

While taking a pause to reflect is important, it is equally important to not get into the analysis paralysis trap of doing postmortems of past decisions and wrong calls. Instead, focusing on the positive aspects of a situation and doing a more appreciative enquiry builds a stronger self-awareness muscle.

Many leaders have specific practices that help them to take out the time for self-reflection. Some build it into their daily routine.

Nirupama and Rajesh have a daily short meditation practice that includes a gratitude and forgiveness meditation. This increases awareness of the positive aspects of life and also builds resilience and optimism. Nirupama does an intention setting exercise before workshops and important conversations where she focuses on what she would like to do and the desired outcome of the intervention.

Deepak Jayaraman, in his book, *Play to Potential*, talks about different types of pauses one can take across four timescales.[47] He practices this and advocates this for leaders.

Hourly for five to ten minutes.

Weekly for around three hours.

Quarterly for a day.
Yearly for about a week.

Ramesh Mangaleswaran makes it a point to take out time for stillness and self-reflection. He started doing Vipassana in 2002. He continues to meditate for 20–40 minutes every day and attends an annual camp for eight to ten days. 'My practice of Vipassana has helped me let go. Vipassana is about what you do every minute of your life. Can you cultivate presence in what you do? It is one thing to be aware and another to be equanimous.' **Mahesh Madhavan** has a regular morning meditation practice. He also practices Kriya Yoga.

Reflection time spent with the energy of gratitude can be enriching and meaningful.

Hephzibah Pathak says, 'I keep space for gratitude, taking time to introspect or journal. It's a powerful ritual. A good way to remind yourself of the good things. It helps reduce anxiety and makes me feel more anchored and joyful.'

Sridhar Balakrishnan, group CEO at Duroflex, has kept a gratitude journal since 2009. He makes a note of everything he can be grateful for. He also makes affirmations that are relevant for him. This, along with a twenty-minute daily meditation, builds deeper self-reflection and awareness.

Mansi Tripathy believes that the *sakshi bhaav*, or the self as witness, is a valuable practice. She is able to observe herself and catch herself before she gets triggered.

Spiritual practices

It is said that faith moves mountains. One way of nurturing the spiritual domain is through spiritual practices that are designed to nurture faith. Irrespective of religion, spiritual practices help us connect to the divine spark within us and outside us. These practices of faith can be great sources of sustenance. Spiritual practices are different from being religious. Religion focuses more upon the specific group and the organization, while spirituality is more generic and may even encompass more than one religious approach.

> Some researchers (Scott, 1997, Zinnbauer, 1997) have found an incredible diversity of definitions among hundreds of study participants, but the main conclusion of one recent meta-analysis has been that 'religion was predominantly associated with formal/organizational religion, while spirituality was more often associated with closeness with God and feelings of interconnectedness with the world and living things'.[48]

Many leaders have spiritual practices that include prayer, chanting, reading spiritual books and listening to spiritual podcasts. **Mahesh Madhavan** derives great comfort from the Bhagavad Gita. ' I take it to heart and practice it in my work.' He also visits temples regularly. **V. Anantha Nageswaran, chief economic adviser to the Government of India,** says, 'I say my daily evening prayers and visit temples whenever the opportunity arises. I do my meditation in the morning with some mudras along with my breathing exercises.'

Mike Spanos, former COO of Delta Airlines and global COO of Bloomin' Brands, upholds Christian values and ethos. He connects these to the workplace, and this helps him function as a 'servant leader' and carry out his mission. **Sivakumar Sundaraman** believes that morning is the most precious part of the day. Instead of waking up to WhatsApp messages or social media, he begins his day with meditation and invoking the divine—a routine that centres the mind and prepares him for a purposeful and fulfilling day.

Ratna Vishwanathan is a practising Buddhist. She follows Nichiren Buddhism, a spiritual practice that works well for her. Earlier, she would take things to heart and get wound up, but this spiritual practice has greatly helped her deal with anxiety and stress.

Vignesh Nandakumar believes that his daily practice of gratitude and meditation, inculcated with the help of coaches, has helped him navigate through tough times. He also picks up something from the Bhagavad Gita regularly and always finds that it gives him the right guidance in each instance. His childhood experience at the Chinmaya Mission has also helped create a life philosophy of 'You should always give more than you take'.

Raghu Krishnan, Area VP, Kenvue, says, 'In a long career, you need something steady to hold on to when things get rough—and for me, that's faith. I take a few minutes each morning to connect with God through a 10-minute prayer/meditation. That simple act helps me put things in perspective and gives me the strength to face whatever the day brings.'

Rajesh also says a short prayer of gratitude and forgiveness every morning and applies *vibhuti*, a smear of sacred ash, on his forehead. This practice makes him feel good and connected to his spirit.

Spiritual practices help us to feel more calm and composed, draw energy from a source greater than ourselves and evoke the positive energies that are needed for us.

Best practices to nurture the spiritual domain

1. **Identify and understand your values:** Identifying your drivers and motivations and ranking them in

order of priorities can be helpful to build alignment. While many people are aware of the values, there can be a difference between espoused values and lived values. Clarity requires introspection. Use some assessment tools like Hogan or Barretts to understand your values.

2. **Create your purpose statement:** Make time and space to create your own purpose statement. Take the help of a coach or mentor to create a personal mission statement that resonates with you. Read the mission statements of other leaders to inspire and guide. Check in often if you are aligned to your purpose and are living your mission.

3. **Find your form of meditation:** The word meditation can be daunting for some people. It is not necessary to sit still for an hour to meditate every day, though many successful leaders do this. Meditation is just a time and way to be still and reflect. Apps like Calm, Headspace and Insight Timer offer a whole range of meditation options from five minutes to longer duration guided meditations. For some people, even activities like running, yoga and walking in nature can be meditative. Find a form that fits you and gives you space and quiet time.

4. **Contribute time and energy to a cause:** Contribution is different from donation. It is not monetary support but support through energy and involvement. Find a cause that you care about. If you are a leader in the corporate world, actively participating in the CSR activities of the organization, such as a volunteering programme or even a simple tree plantation drive, will offer a sense of contribution. You could also do some pro bono mentoring for young leaders

or those who do not have access to professional guidance.
5. **Follow your faith:** Your faith becomes your courage touchstone. You do not have to follow organized religion, be devoted to a particular god or follow a guru. Even if you are a non-believer, anyone or anything can become your spiritual guide. Nature and the vast wonders of the universe can be a source of faith. The belief in the human spirit and goodness of humanity can be a beacon during dark days. For some, it is a personal philosophy or certain tenets that they live by. For example, stoicism and humanism of existentialism can also be sources of inspiration and meaning.

ENRICH YOUR SOUL

- IDENTIFY YOUR VALUES

 - CREATE YOUR PURPOSE STATEMENT

- FIND YOUR FORM OF MEDITATION

 - CONTRIBUTE TO A CAUSE

- FOLLOW YOUR FAITH

Section III

Growing Others

8

Nurture Others

'Management is about arranging and telling. Leadership is about nurturing and enhancing.'

—Tom Peters

'Leadership is not about being in charge. It's about taking care of those in our charge.'

—Simon Sinek, *Leaders Eat Last*

Nurturing others refers to leadership at work. In the days of the Industrial Revolution and early stages of the Technological Revolution, it was enough to ensure that employees were productive and not disgruntled. The demand and supply equation was in favour of the employer rather than the employee, and employees were satisfied with decent wages and working conditions. Humans were seen as resources, a term that continues even today to describe the function that is responsible for people management. Resources are used, even exploited, to serve a particular goal.

Now, leadership is more than just aligning the team to achieve organizational goals. With the advance of automation and artificial intelligence, most of the routine tasks are done by smart machines. Organizations need people who are creative, agile, can take ownership and accountability and demonstrate leadership qualities at an early stage. Leaders want creativity and commitment, not just compliance. Policies and processes are designed around people rather than the other way around.

The new world of work needs leaders who can nurture and bring out the best in others. If we extend our leader-as-a-gardener metaphor here, the leader needs to tend to the organization and people in a way that lets them grow and bloom.

Magdalena Nowicka Mook, CEO of the International Coaching Federation, says that the modern workplace needs a modern style of leadership. A good leader needs to know the team well, support them through tough times and allow for participative decision-making.

Radhika Gupta says, 'There is a lot of stress. Leadership is not about flying around in a cape. Leaders need to share the burden.'

This can happen only if leaders nurture others.

Prakash Iyer, motivational speaker, author of several books and former MD of Kimberly Clark, says, 'You usually don't associate the word "nurturing" with leadership. It is important to go beyond driving results. What makes a leader a great leader is no longer about delivering on last quarter's profits; it is about the impact we leave on people. Who would want to have coffee with me when I am no longer in a position of authority? It is probably the people whom I have nurtured through the years.'

Leaders who are secure and confident in themselves become nurturers of the talent and potential of others.

Anil Arjun, CEO of Storiculture, believes that it is important to humanize people and look beyond their CVs and job descriptions. The modern workplace has been about combat and competition. This does not bring out the best in people. **Vikas Srivastava, ex MD, Johnson & Johnson Consumer (India),** says, 'Leaders need to be strategic about nurturing others. One of the credo values of J&J is employee well-being, and this has helped me ingrain nurturing others into my DNA.'

Vineet Nayar, former CEO of HCL Technologies, advocates the mindset of 'Employee First, Customer Second', also the name of his book. By taking care of your employees, you can ensure that they take care of the customers.

We believe that nurturing the self as well as others needs to start at an early stage, not just when you become a CEO. Many of the leaders shared that they were able to handle the CEO role well, as nurturing the self and others was a practice they had followed for several years.

We will examine three aspects of nurturing others: the process of nurturing, the qualities required to be a nurturing leader and the nurturing behaviours. While process sets the stage, qualities support behaviours and behaviours finally lead to results. We will deep dive into the behaviours since these will help to understand the best practices of Nurturing Leadership in a better way.

The process of nurturing

Since the process of nurturing is most often associated with growing living things, we thought it most appropriate to continue with our gardener/farmer analogy. Even though we may say, 'It is a jungle out there!', an organization is more like a garden or orchard than a forest. A forest grows by itself, without the intention or intervention of any human. A garden or an orchard needs to be planned, tended, cared for and nurtured towards a particular end—to yield flowers or fruits.

Sometimes, a leader takes over a garden that has already grown into a shape and form. Sometimes, a founder/leader dreams of and then builds a new garden. Whichever stage of growth the organization is in, the nurturing leader follows a process.

THE PROCESS OF NURTURING OTHERS

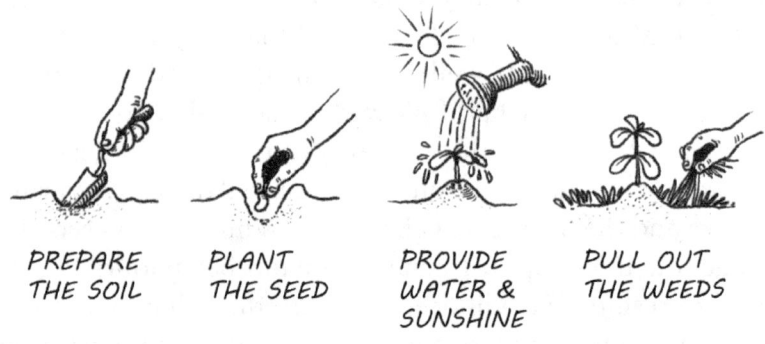

PREPARE THE SOIL   PLANT THE SEED   PROVIDE WATER & SUNSHINE   PULL OUT THE WEEDS

Prepare the soil

Before planting any new seeds, the soil needs to be prepared. Healthy soil is a living, dynamic ecosystem. The right plant can die in the wrong soil. Preparing the soil is not a one-time activity. Gardeners recommend turning the soil over at least once a year. Turning over the soil helps in better aeration and root penetration and allows the plant to absorb the water and nutrients in a better way. Sometimes, the hard soil needs to be broken up. Customs, policies and processes that have become outmoded and behaviours that don't serve the purpose any longer need to be phased out. New fertilizer may need to be added to the soil.

The mission, vision, values and culture impact the environment of the organization and leaders need to understand and reinforce these. Employees need to be supported by the right policies and processes that can help them to perform at their best. During the Covid-19 years, many policies needed to be changed to allow employees to work from home. Once the dangers of the pandemic had passed, many organizations wanted employees to come back to work and be physically present in the office. Some organizations still operate on a hybrid model. The leader has to take the call on what best serves and balances the needs of the individual and the organization.

'Mission clarity—the what—and strategy breakdown—the how—aren't just management jargon. They're what breathes life into our values. It's how values move from being posters on the wall to becoming part of how we work, what we celebrate and how we hold ourselves accountable. That's what creates the environment where individuals thrive—and when individuals thrive, the organization wins,' says **Yamini Bhat**.

When **Rajesh** moved to Bangladesh as the MD of Perfetti Van Melle, the garden had a form but was in need of attention and had the potential to grow. The soil needed to be turned, and the mission needed to be articulated and communicated to create the right environment for growth. The right plants had to be planted and the weeds had to be removed. Rajesh, along with his management committee, had to provide the right level of sunshine and water to allow the plants to grow and the flowers to bloom. The results were there for all to see—the garden thrived and the business started to flourish.

Plant the seeds

If a leader is a founder, building a new organization from the beginning, hiring the right people is the most important aspect of the role. It is important to choose the people who will flourish in the soil that you have created. There is no point in expecting a rose to grow in the desert soil or a cactus in a tropical rainforest. As an organization grows, there will always be new seeds to be planted along the way.

Anil Arjun says, 'I hire for vibes. I look beyond the CV and job experience, education and other markers to see if the person can contribute and thrive in our environment.'

A beautiful garden has a variety of plants and flowers, each bringing their unique colour, fragrance and form. Nurturing leaders believe in the benefits of diversity and bring this perspective while choosing people. Each employee brings their unique combination of energy, skills and time and nurturing leaders respect them for that. Nurturing leaders allow for diversity and are inclusive in the selection approach. The leader must ensure that they manage their conscious and unconscious biases and remain objective as they hire, promote and grow their people.

Planting the seeds is also about enabling people to think creatively, come up with their own ideas and shine on their own. The leader can plant the seeds of an idea or give a broad direction, but if they have the loudest voice in the room, the employee will not be able to develop, just as plants cannot grow to their full potential under the shade of a large tree.

Provide water and sunshine

Once the planting has been done, the work of the gardener begins in earnest. A plant cannot grow in a dark, dry corner.

Without the right amount of light and liquid, they fade away and perish.

Here is where experience and discernment matter the most. A gardener cannot treat all plants the same way. A snake plant may thrive in less light, in a cool corner of the living room but a petunia needs the direct light of the sun to bloom. Leaders need to understand the needs of the employee and flex their style accordingly. All plants need some amount of water and sunshine but how much, how long and how often will differ. The leader needs to know who needs more coaching, who can be trusted to do the job entirely on their own, who needs more appreciation, who needs more constructive feedback and who wants to be left alone for the most part.

The work of providing daily nurturing is not that of the CEO alone. Anyone who is a leader of others has this responsibility for another's career growth. Water and sunshine need to be provided consistently for people and plants to grow.

Pull out the weeds

All plants do not swiftly and seamlessly grow to bear flowers and fruit. They may be attacked by pests, develop some disease, get eaten by an animal or damaged by heavy rains. The beautiful garden could be overrun by weeds. A good gardener will pull out the weeds, put up a stake or make a scarecrow. A leader may sometimes need to take a strong call. You thought someone was a plant, but he turned out to be a weed. Maybe you brought the wrong seeds. Instead of the magical beanstalk you expected, you were growing poison ivy. It is time to weed out what is not working. An employee who is unethical, non-compliant or just badly behaved needs to be dealt with accordingly.

Weeds can overrun the whole garden if you don't pull them out in time. Leaders need to find the balance between giving people the benefit of doubt and calling out blatant bad behaviours.

Leaders also nurture by holding a mirror to the team member, which enables them to also see their blind spots. Interferences, both external and internal, need to be weeded out from the individual and the system. Trees and shrubs are pruned regularly to remove dead, diseased or damaged branches that could be a safety risk. A nurturing leader does not shy away from constructive feedback and challenging the team member to correct dysfunctional behaviours.

These steps are essential to nurture a beautiful garden. But the garden will be as wonderful as the gardener. While the leaders need to nurture themselves, they also need certain qualities that can enable nurturing. These qualities will enable the nurturing behaviours needed to be demonstrated on a consistent basis.

The qualities of nurturing leaders are supported by a growth mindset instead of a fixed mindset. This allows them to explore possibilities to make things happen. The concept of the growth mindset was first introduced by eminent psychologist Carol Dweck in her research on achievement and success. In her 2006 book, *Mindset: The New Psychology of Success*,[49] Dweck describes the growth mindset as a belief that talents, intelligence and abilities can be developed through dedication, effort and learning from feedback. This contrasts with the fixed mindset, which is the belief that abilities and intelligence are static and cannot be changed significantly. Leaders with a fixed mindset believe that their employees cannot grow, cannot learn new skills and are not capable of taking on new challenges.

Leaders with a growth mindset believe that many of the abilities can be cultivated. They see challenges as growth opportunities and often persevere through them as part of their learning process. This can often be infectious and motivates others to follow a similar approach, leading to the overall bar of the organization going up. Such leaders also tend to set learning goals that are focused on improvement as opposed to performance goals, which are only based on outcomes and on proving one's abilities.

In their study titled 'Growth Mindset in Leaders and Employee Development',[50] Peter Heslin and Don Vandewalle studied the impact of managers' mindsets on their approach to employee development. Managers with a growth mindset believed that employees' abilities could be developed, while those with a fixed mindset tended to see employee skills as stable traits.

The key findings were around how managers with a growth mindset were more likely to engage in behaviours that fostered employee development, such as offering feedback, coaching and career guidance. They viewed setbacks as opportunities for learning rather than as failures, which encouraged employees to pursue growth. This study suggests that managers with a growth mindset are more nurturing and supportive of their employees, helping them build skills and confidence, ultimately leading to a more positive and productive workplace.

This requires the four qualities of **humility, openness, patience and empathy (HOPE)**. HOPE is the foundational building block that leads to nurturing. The gardener cannot demand or expect that the plant will grow exactly in a particular way. Unlike a building that we can create to exact specifications, nature does not follow a predictable path. A parent can only provide all the love and care needed for a child, but there is no way to predict what your child will grow up to become or the exact kind of life they will have. Do your best and hope for the best holds true for people and for plants.

The qualities of HOPE support a leader with a growth mindset in growing the employees. Even in the most structured organization with strictly defined processes and policies, people do not behave or perform exactly according to expectations. They grow in different ways. They don't respond well to fear, threats or coercion, especially in the long run.

These qualities hold true across geographies, industries and generations and lead to nurturing behaviours.

THE QUALITIES FOR NURTURING OTHERS

HUMILITY   OPENNESS   PATIENCE   EMPATHY

Humility: The pace of change is at lightspeed. What the leader knew to be true yesterday need not be so tomorrow. Therefore, it is important to be humble and teachable as a leader. Leaders who are humble appreciate the fact that they do not have all the answers. They need to get the best out of others. Others can be smarter and more knowledgeable than them in many domains. An arrogant leader will look to protect his turf and stifle others instead of giving them space to grow and flourish.

Retired Vice Admiral Anil Kumar Chawla believes that humility is important as you grow higher in your career. This helps you forgive your own mistakes and those of others and also learn from them.

Ayushi Gudwani feels that humility is a great enabler to learning.

Prakash Iyer says, 'As a young manager, I would try to fill in the blanks for others and rush to provide solutions. People like to say "I know" and then show that they know. It is more powerful to ask, "What do you think?" Humility is the quality that enables you to do that.'

Openness: Leaders need to be open to change and challenge. A leader who is open to receiving different ideas and views can encourage people to contribute and share openly. This in turn fosters trust, creates psychological safety and leads to greater creativity and productivity. Openness also helps to enhance diversity and build inclusive teams.

Hemant Malik approaches each day as a new learning. His mindset of curiosity and openness helps to engage with each interaction and each challenge with fresh energy.

'Accessibility and openness are important,' says **Vivek Gambhir**. 'I don't say "no" to requests for meetings. I am curious and learn from each interaction.'

Curiosity leads to being open to new ideas and opinions different from your own and to truly wanting to know the other person's story. Leaders also need to be open to receiving. Can you receive an idea that is contrary to yours? Can you receive feedback with grace? Can you receive feedback from a junior person?

Amrita Randhawa teaches people to tell their own stories. This leads to more openness and authenticity, which can be very empowering.

Openness is different from agreeing with or accepting another's ideas and thoughts. Some leaders may think of openness as making you look indecisive or weak. They think that if you don't push your agenda or thoughts aggressively, it will not be taken seriously. This actually prevents new ideas and new ways of doing things. Leaders who are closed also end up closing the business.

Patience: Patience is the most underrated leadership quality. Successful leaders are seen as anything but patient. Our global work culture thrives on speed, agility and quick results. Impatience is seen as the hallmark of a good leader and patience is the burden that a 'loser' has to carry.

However, patience is key to being a nurturing leader. People cannot grow overnight. Nor can you force them to quickly fulfil their potential. Having the discernment to know when to push and when to be patient is important. Patience helps you understand timing. This helps one in making effective decisions that are well thought out rather than rushed decisions under the guise of agility.

Patience is important for effective listening. Most people don't have the patience to let another person complete a sentence before airing their point of view. Patience allows you to listen fully and frame powerful questions based on the insights gathered. Patience is not passivity. It is about being more deliberate and purposeful and allowing things that take time to actually take their time.

Would you inject steroids into your children to make them grow faster? Your toddler will not turn into a teenager until his or her time has come. Until then, the parent needs patience.

Patience can be learnt. **Uday Sinha** says that playing golf has taught him patience. He knows that the bad days on the course and in life will pass. **Kaushik Mukherjee** has also learnt patience in his entrepreneurial role. He feels that equanimity has made him more stable and grounded.

Empathy: The ability to understand another's thoughts and feelings and offer support according to their needs is empathy in action. Without this discernment and connection, it is not possible to nurture others. Empathy is important for all leaders but critical in certain sectors that are highly people-focused.

Ram Raghavan defines empathy as the ability to put yourself in someone else's shoes, but you need to take your shoes off first. **Dr Parag Rindani** feels that the quality of empathy is on a decline. In the healthcare industry, it directly affects the quality of patient care.

Hina Nagarajan says, 'Leading with empathy goes beyond having a positive impact on people. It impacts innovation, engagement and retention and fosters an inclusive workforce, all leading to better business performance.' Empathy fuels care and compassion, which help nurture others. Without genuine care and empathy, there cannot be authentic connections and a sense of trust in a team.

We explore empathy in detail in the chapter on Listening.

Qualities are demonstrated through behaviours. The qualities of HOPE help us in mentoring and coaching, inspiring, listening and empowering (MILE) others. These qualities and behaviours are required through the entire process of nurturing, from preparing the soil to pulling out weeds. The behaviours can be demonstrated skilfully by effective leaders or ineffectively. We believe all the behaviours of nurturing leaders can be learnt and implemented. While leaders may do one or the other of these, we believe that all aspects of MILE are important to nurture others.

THE BEHAVIOURS FOR NURTURING OTHERS

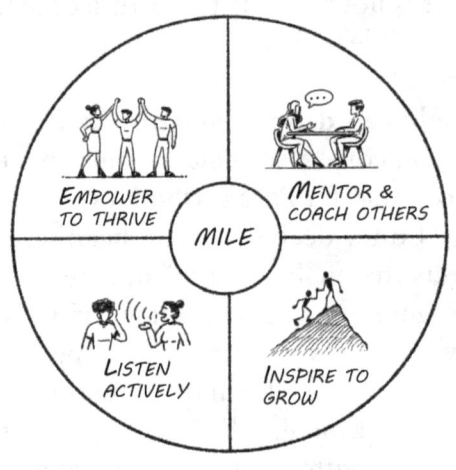

9

Mentor and Coach Others

'Mentoring is a brain to pick, an ear to listen, and a push in the right direction.'

—John C. Crosby

'That's the beauty of coaching. You get to touch lives. You get to make a difference.'

—Morgan Wootten

Mentoring and coaching provide the water and sunshine needed by people at different stages in the employee life cycle. The leaders who are skilled in mentoring and coaching can support the team to grow. Sometimes, through these behaviours, they can also help to pull out the weeds and shine a light on the blind spots or dark areas that a person may not be aware of.

Effective mentoring and coaching can benefit the mentee/coachee, mentor/coach and the organization at large. Workplace mentoring programmes help in cultivating strong relationships among employees and increase the overall productivity of the workforce. They help build a strong, inclusive culture in the organization. They also help bring down attrition and help build smart succession plans.

According to a 2016 Gallup survey, mentored employees reported higher engagement levels because they feel supported and valued within the organization.[51]

One interesting aspect we observed was that leaders referred to mentoring and coaching interchangeably, even though they are different. In this chapter, we will delve into understanding the definition of mentoring and coaching, the role of a leader as a mentor and coach, the impact of mentoring and coaching on the team members and the best practices on how to be an effective coach and mentor.

Mentoring

The word mentor comes from Greek mythology, where Mentor was a senior statesperson and friend of the king Odysseus. He was supposed to provide guidance and support to Telemachus, the young son of Odysseus, after he left for his travels.

Mentoring is the process in which someone shares their knowledge, skills, experience and wisdom with another person to help them to progress. A mentor is typically someone senior with valuable insights and experience who offers guidance and support.

We also need to make a distinction between mentoring conversations and mentoring relationships. Conversations where the leader shares their knowledge and experience, life stories and helps the mentee feel confident, empowered and skilled are valuable. This can be a one-off conversation or organic conversations when someone approaches the leader for guidance.

Mentoring relationships require more investment and energy from the leader. This is a longer-term relationship where a leader has a genuine interest in the growth and development of the mentee. The leader as mentor then grooms the mentee over a period of time. Many leaders do mentor a successor or a second-level leader to enhance their potential.

Most of the leaders we spoke to mentor employees from within the organization. Some of them do take out time to offer guidance, advice and be a sounding board for former team members and others who approach them.

Effective mentors can help you connect the dots that you are unable to see because you are too close to the dots. They can step in to give clarity and confidence for you to move forward in your work.

There are various models for mentoring that talk about the different stages of the mentoring process.

Informal mentoring happens organically when a leader engages with a team member and passes on knowledge and gives guidance beyond what is required to get the job done. Mentors can also share their knowledge of the organizational system and help employees navigate their careers. This can happen through sporadic conversations over a period of time, where the mentor and mentee have an understanding about the nature of their relationship.

Formal mentoring is a more structured process. Nirupama has supported many organizations to run internal mentoring programmes as a part of leadership development. Mentoring is seen as a critical skill for leaders to work on.

In a structured mentoring programme, leaders are paired with usually junior employees who are assigned to them as mentees.

Structured mentoring conversations usually have four stages: rapport building, goal setting, making progress and wrapping up. We will examine each of these in some detail.

Rapport building: The stage in which a space of mutual trust and respect is created and built upon. This requires the mentor to demonstrate deep listening, empathy and curiosity. This stage lays the foundation for a successful mentoring relationship.

Goal setting: Once the rapport is built, the next stage is about setting clear objectives or goals that need to be achieved during the engagement. This is also the time to set clear expectations from each other.

Making progress: This stage is where the mentee gets the maximum value in terms of insights, learning and development. The mentor may share personal examples to further build trust and also provide insights to the mentee. It is also a good time to challenge the mentee on their thinking and help them look at things from different perspectives. This stage helps the mentee build their resilience and self-confidence.

Wrapping up: As the objectives are met, this is where the relationship starts naturally winding down. This is a good time for the mentor to check in with the mentee in terms of achievement of objectives and for the mentee to express gratitude to the mentor.

The process of mentoring individuals is a great way to nurture them. This can have a positive cascading effect in the organization.

Narasimhan Eswar says, 'I spend a lot of time mentoring my team. I ensure that we have a clearly aligned vision, I equip them with the relevant tools and resources and I keep a watch on them from the sidelines.'

Both informal and formal mentoring are ways of nurturing and developing employees. Leaders who mentor well can leave a lasting impact on the people they engage with. Some of the people mentored by the leaders also shared their experiences.

Aparna M. Vishwasrao, CHRO of USV Pvt Ltd, says, 'Apurva, true to her name (which denotes unique in Sanskrit), is a unique mentor. She has guided me both on the developmental side to improve a few aspects of my leadership skills and, at a practical level, shown me how to navigate through the choppy waters of senior and top management roles. I realized that I could be empathetic and collaborative yet make firm decisions, observing her style. As I was evolving as a leader over the years, **Apurva Purohit** has been a guiding post and a beacon of hope through her one-on-one mentoring sessions.'

Rachna Kanwar, COO Digital Media, Radio City and Mid-Day Mumbai, goes on to add, '**Apurva Purohit** has profoundly influenced my professional journey and personal growth throughout my years at Radio City and Mid-Day. In my early years, I was deeply impacted by her concept of "tough love", and it has become the bedrock of team management for me. As a woman leader, I learnt to nurture and support younger women and prepare them for leadership roles.'

Vipul Sabharwal, former CEO of Luminous Power Technologies, talks about how he has benefited from the mentoring of **Shiv Shivakumar,** 'Shiv Shivakumar is very versatile as a leader and a good assessor of people. He adapts his mentoring style to suit the needs of the individual. Shiv also shares a lot of his learnings and knowledge very happily and openly and this has immensely benefited me.'

Nupur Goenka, leadership consultant and executive coach, echoes the sentiment. She says, 'It feels like Shiv brings the entire width and depth of his experiences and principles to the table when he's coaching us; there's so much knowledge and thinking to share, but he always provokes us to apply our own styles, contexts, and value systems. He has always strongly encouraged authenticity and calls out what he sees as our strengths and gives us ideas on how to leverage it. But most importantly, we have built a foundation of trust because of his style of candour with care. Shiv has a way of calling out behaviours and actions that he feels could be unproductive or destructive in a way that you walk away both inspired and energised to make changes rather than feel crippled. He has become someone whose wisdom and advice we have relied on for our trickiest situations.'

In some cases, the mentoring relationship can also lead to sponsorship, where the mentor actively advocates and champions the cause of the mentee for key roles and responsibilities. **Pranab Barua** says, 'I nurture others through active mentoring. I find being empathetic and listening well is more than half the job. I also learn a lot from my mentees in the process, especially digital marketing, social media impact and the use of AI in running businesses more effectively.'

Another aspect that is gaining popularity these days among senior leaders is the concept of reverse mentoring. Reverse mentoring is where the younger person shares their knowledge and skills, often in the areas of technology and ways of thinking of the new generation, with the more senior folks. The former CEO of General Electric, Jack Welch, is credited with inventing the concept of reverse mentoring. He recognized his lack of technology skills in the late 1990s and believed that the youngest people joining the company were far more knowledgeable about new technologies than their managers. So he asked 500 of his top executives to seek out mentors from among these new joiners.

Some organizations have started taking a more structured approach to reverse mentoring and have begun to embed it as part of their DNA. **C.V.L. Srinivas** says, 'We set up reverse mentoring in our organization; we created a "shadow board", which helps senior leaders be up to date on what the younger generations are thinking, and it also gives the youth in the organization a voice on the table.'

Coaching

John Whitmore, one of the eminent leadership development experts, once said, 'Coaching is unlocking people's potential to maximize their own performance. It is more often helping them to learn rather than teaching them.'

The main focus of coaching is to help individuals discover their full potential. Coaching is often provided to a person on a one-on-one basis by a qualified coach. A knowledgeable coach leverages various tools and techniques, generally through a structured programme, to achieve desired objectives. According to the International Coach Federation (ICF), coaching is defined as 'partnering with clients in a thought-provoking and creative process that inspires them to maximize their personal and professional potential.'

Magdalena Nowicka Mook makes a clear distinction between the work of a professional certified coach and the use of coaching skills by operational leaders and managers. 'Leaders are not expected to be professional coaches—they do need to use coaching skills in the conversations they have with their teams. In order for leaders to be effective, they would do well to leverage key coaching skills like empathy, deep listening and asking powerful questions.'

Daniel Goleman identified the coaching style as one of the six key leadership styles that are used, especially by leaders who want to foster the growth and development of their teams.

Ruchira Chaudhary's book *Coaching: The Secret Code to Uncommon Leadership* is a great resource for any leader who want to use coaching to nurture talent. 'A truly uncommon and extraordinary leader is one that coaches—a process whereby a coach/leader aims to maximize the performance and potential of others through nondirective, self-enabling conversations. The uncommon leader elevates and empowers their people, and in doing so, elevates themselves.'[52]

She has created a 4C+ model, which identifies key coaching outcomes for leaders as they coach their teams- Capability, Consciousness, Confidence and Clarity.

In a typical coaching conversation, irrespective of the kind of coaching, the role of the coach is to ask powerful questions, listen with empathy and go deeper to help the coachee come up with insights that help them achieve their desired goals.

Leaders can use coaching skills to get the best out of their employees. When a leader refrains from giving their own solutions and allows for the team member to discover the answer, they are using coaching skills.

Leaders may coach informally, in the corridor or during a cab ride or structure a more formal 1:1 session with their teams. I, Nirupama, remember going with my mentor and previous boss at AchieveGlobal, Michael Griffin, on sales calls to customers. He would coach me on the way to the client by asking questions about my objective, strategy and approach.

Aditya Sehgal says, 'I ask people the right questions and let them discover their own solutions and learnings.' Asking powerful questions, avoiding advice and deep listening are the ways in which leaders can coach people to enhance their potential.

Mohit Sadaani also believes that he has a coaching style of leadership. ' I give people space. I ask a lot of questions and help them to figure out stuff.'

Arnab Banerjee, MD and CEO of CEAT Tyres, is a big believer in coaching to nurture the self and others. He says, 'I am a certified coach, and I actively coach people within and outside my organization. Coaching helps others operate to their full potential, and it also improves me as a person.'

Geetika Mehta uses coaching and mentoring effectively to nurture others. She says, 'I invest my time in coaching people across the organization, I provide them psychological safety and actively listen with empathy.'

I, Rajesh, started on my coaching journey when I was MD at Perfetti Van Melle, and the idea was to coach people in the organization and pay it forward. I actively coach people both within and outside the organization. I find the process extremely satisfying and fulfilling. Coaching helped me become a better listener and further increased my levels of empathy.

Mayank Pandey, country manager Nepal, Perfetti Van Melle, had this to say, 'I have worked with Rajesh as a part of his team since 2019. During this time, Rajesh has been more of a mentor and inspiration than a manager. What really made Rajesh a great mentor and coach were his empathy, encouraging us to build a learning mindset and deep commitment to the growth and well-being of his team. Rajesh invested a significant amount of time and energy to share perspectives, examples and insights into what I must learn and unlearn to not only hone my general management skills but also become a genuine human being and team player.'

Vineet Sharma, GM and senior director, franchise-AMESA-Pepsi Lipton JV, goes on to add, 'Rajesh has been my mentor since 2008, when he was my manager. In the last year, he coached me on identifying the purpose and mission for myself. His sessions helped me discover the true purpose of who I want to be. This enabled me to prioritize and focus on what really matters and be comfortable with my choices since they are unique to me. It also focused me on career choices that play to my strengths and are also enriching for me, as they align with my values in life.'

Mentoring versus coaching

Many leaders end up using the terms mentoring and coaching interchangeably. While there are some similarities between the two, there are also some fundamental differences. We will examine some of these to get a deeper understanding of these two concepts.

Some of the similarities between mentoring and coaching are as follows:

- Both processes are based on the principles of mutual trust and respect.
- Both rely on building one-on-one relationships.
- Both processes require the mentor/coach to be empathetic and a good listener.
- Both processes require commitment from both parties.
- Successful mentors/coaches tend to be adaptable and intuitive.

There are also some key differences between the two as listed below:

- Coaching is usually goal oriented and works even in the short term while mentoring is a longer relationship.
- Coaching is about getting the solutions from the coachee while mentoring is about giving the appropriate guidance.
- Coaching usually follows a structured approach, while mentoring is more free-flowing.
- Coaching is used to enhance performance and potential and therefore is more evaluative and measurable, while mentoring is largely non-evaluative and developmental

Mentoring and coaching requires commitment from leaders in terms of investing their time, effort and energy into it. Leaders need to see this as part of their job and not something that they do 'in addition'. Done well, this can be very rewarding and can have a cascading impact on the organization as well. **Sanjiv Mehta** says, 'I used to set aside the time between 8 a.m. and 9 a.m. for meeting with people for any mentoring that they might seek. It is important to make time for people, listen well and put the entire focus on that issue of that person.' Says **Neil George,** 'I set aside every Saturday morning from 7 a.m. for my mentoring conversations. People call to discuss various topics, including career advice, tough bosses and even personal development. I do this almost every Saturday, and it is extremely fulfilling.'

Ram Raghavan leverages existing processes to embed mentoring in the organization. He says, 'I encourage my team members to pick one trait per year that they would like to work on, keeping the future in mind, then have a specific action plan and take regular feedback on the progress.'

Impact of mentoring and coaching on leaders

As mentioned by various leaders, mentoring and coaching, apart from nurturing others, can significantly enhance key leadership competencies in leaders and help them on their own leadership journey. Mentors often improve their communication, leadership and interpersonal skills. (Bozeman & Feeney, 2007).[53] Other areas that get positively impacted for mentors are time management, active listening, adaptability, empathy and patience.

Mentoring and coaching also helps leaders form deeper connections with people in the organization. It makes them more accessible and approachable. It can also be a strong asset for senior leaders as they transition from full-time work to the next chapter in their lives.

Research has shown that people who served as mentors experienced less anxiety and described their jobs as more meaningful than those who did not mentor.[54]

A 2015 study by Gallup[55] found that managers who take a coaching approach (focusing on employees' strengths and development) result in 21 per cent higher productivity and 65 per cent lower turnover. Employees coached by leaders reported higher levels of trust, loyalty and motivation.

Mentoring and coaching can be used very effectively in an entrepreneurial context as well to groom and develop young talent. In an entrepreneurial setup, there is an increased need to navigate through uncharted territories. The workforce in startups is also relatively younger. Mentoring can play a key role here to effectively nurture talent. **Hitesh Oberoi** likes to bet on young talent. He says, 'I identify and empower young talent and give them opportunities and mentor them over time. Many of my senior leaders have been with us for twelve to fifteen years—the company has done well, and they have also grown with the company.'

Ramesh Mangaleswaran sums it up well: 'Mentoring and coaching can be a very powerful tool in the hands of leaders. By effectively using them, leaders can enable people to find their larger purpose in life and at work, help them amplify their strengths and work around their limitations.'

Best practices for mentoring and coaching

1. **Ask powerful questions:** Asking the right questions is a key aspect of effective coaching. Don't jump to provide solutions; allow them to figure it out for themselves. Leaders need the qualities of openness and humility to ask questions that come from a place of wanting to know more rather than waiting to tell more.
2. **Set aside time:** A few words of advice during a corridor catch-up is not mentoring. Block time at a certain periodicity for mentoring and coaching conversations. This will help leaders practice this on an ongoing basis. If there is no time set aside for this, mentoring is not effective. Intention alone is not enough. Impact comes through deliberate actions.
3. **Embed in the organization:** Create an ecosystem in the organization where coaching and mentoring become part of the culture. Leverage existing processes to embed mentoring and coaching in the organization. Make coaching a part of your leadership style.
4. **Keep it receiver focused:** Just sharing your experiences with everyone is not mentoring or coaching. Tailor your approach to the person on the other end. Does this team member need more of Telling/Sharing or

Asking/Listening? Does the person need a Push or a Pull? Adapt your approach accordingly.
5. **Be authentic:** People will not change in a moment or in a day. Coaching is a process that requires consistency and investment. Be your authentic self so that others can learn and grow. Don't lose hope just because you have not created a magical transformation through a single conversation.

MENTOR & COACH OTHERS

• ASK POWERFUL QUESTIONS

 • SET ASIDE TIME

• EMBED IN THE ORGANIZATION

 • KEEP IT STRUCTURED

• BE AUTHENTIC

10

Inspire to Grow

'Average leaders raise the bar on themselves; good leaders raise the bar for others; great leaders inspire others to raise their own bar.'

—Orrin Woodward

Adam Grant said, 'Good leaders build products. Great leaders build cultures. Good leaders deliver results. Great leaders develop people. Good leaders have vision. Great leaders have values. Good leaders are role models at work. Great leaders are role models in life.'

This quote sums up the various facets of an inspiring leader. Inspiring leaders leave behind a legacy long after they are gone. A part of the legacy is about the impact that they have on the business, but the larger legacy is usually to do with their impact on the people and the community at large.

Inspiration refers to the process of being mentally or emotionally stimulated to feel, think or act in a way that leads to creativity, motivation or positive change.

The behaviours we relate to inspiring are also required at the different processes of nurturing. Inspiration can be a powerful impetus for growth.

While leaders can be inspiring in many ways, we will focus on the aspects of inspiration that lead to nurturing others. The concept of 'Lovemarks' was introduced by Kevin Roberts, former CEO of Saatchi & Saatchi, in his 2004 book *Lovemarks: The Future Beyond Brands*.[56] Lovemarks refers to brands that inspire 'loyalty beyond reason' by forming emotional connections with consumers through love, respect and storytelling. These brands go beyond traditional brand loyalty by creating a sense of belonging and emotional resonance.

This concept can be extrapolated to leaders as well. Inspiring leaders are usually looked up to and respected for their knowledge, experience and wisdom—all key dimensions of respect. However, inspiring leaders who are also good at nurturing their team bring in an additional dimension of love; they demonstrate and inculcate behaviours such as authenticity, compassion, empathy and vulnerability. When you layer on the dimension of compelling storytelling to this, you have truly inspiring and nurturing leaders—Lovemarks in their own right.

Inspiring leaders are good at nurturing themselves, but they are even better at nurturing others. They have this innate ability to inspire and nurture their team. They create a compelling vision and motivate themselves and others to achieve stretch goals through their words, actions and behaviour. They are self-aware, passionate, empathetic and committed to guiding and nurturing others. They know that working together is key to success, and hence they focus their energies on bringing the best out of others by giving them purpose and fulfilment.

All of us can think of some inspiring leaders who we have looked up to and learnt from, things that stand us in good stead even today. That is the power of an inspiring leader—they make an impact that can last a lifetime.

While this impact can be at a professional level, by way of the business lessons we imbibe while working with them, it's usually more at a personal level where they help us grow into better human beings.

One of the leaders who inspired me to grow my practice of supporting women, was Sheryl Sandberg, the former COO of Facebook. She did not stop with just a TED talk and a book, *Lean In*. She set up an organization and a movement around the book which supports thousands of other women. After I wrote my book, *Powerful: The Indian Woman's Guide to Unlocking Her Full Potential*, I was inspired to extend it beyond a book to an assessment tool and a whole system, which could enhance the power quotient of women in India.[57] Today, I can proudly say that the Powerfulife system has positively impacted thousands of women in the country.

Inspiring starts with creating a solid vision and mission for the organization and communicating them effectively. Even if visions and mission statements have been set by someone else, a nurturing leader communicates them both clearly and consistently. This is what prepares the soil for people to thrive. A leader who can create and communicate an inspiring vision will lay the foundation for exponential growth. It was Nelson Mandela's vision for a society without discrimination, where all the people were equal and free, that inspired an entire nation to follow the path of reconciliation rather than revenge.

The soil cannot be prepared just once with the establishment of the vision, mission and values. These need to be reiterated and reinforced visibly and consistently, just as the soil needs to be turned again and again.

We also see the need for inspiring behaviours as a leader plants the seeds of an idea in the people. Through the inspiring behaviours, the leader is an active role model who can grow and shape people.

We have identified three distinct behaviors of leaders who inspire others to grow.

Raise the bar

President John F. Kennedy's vision of sending a man to the moon helped marshal all the resources available in the USA to make this vision come true. In Kennedy's words,

> We choose to go to the moon in this decade and do the other things, not because they are easy, but because they are hard, because that goal will serve to organize and measure the best of our energies and skills, because that challenge is one that we are willing to accept, one we are unwilling to postpone, and one which we intend to win, and the others, too.[58]

A nurturing leader who believes in the team is able to raise the bar for everyone's performance.

Kalpesh Parmar says, 'Start behaving like you're already at the level you want to get to. Raise the bar. Elevate yourself first.' **B. Govindarajan** shares, 'I push people to come up with breakthrough ideas rather than incremental ones. I learn new things like AI, workshop with the team and grow along with them.'

Inspirational leaders set very high standards for themselves and constantly strive to achieve their stretch goals. They are always seeking innovative ways of doing things and often take themselves outside their comfort zone.

Supported by a growth mindset, leaders who inspire also tend to have higher expectations from those around them.

The Pygmalion Effect is a psychological phenomenon where people perform better when they are expected to perform better.[59] When these expectations are communicated to team members, they adapt their behaviours to match the expectations, in the process delivering better results. Such leaders who have high expectations from their teams tend to enhance the self-esteem of the team and boost their confidence, leading to resilience and perseverance. This motivates the team to learn and grow.

This in turn has a cascading effect across the organization and the productivity of the organization goes up. However, inspiring leaders also ensure that they are there to provide the adequate support for their teams both physically and emotionally to help them achieve their goals and prevent burnout. **Alok Mittal** inspires his team to go for stretch goals and supports them to achieve it by creating a safe space for failing, learning and growing.

Malika Datt Sadaani also sets a high standard, inspiring her team to learn and grow. She invests in individuals who demonstrate drive, ambition and a strong desire to succeed. **Harit Nagpal** adds, 'I set standards that are high to help build leaders. This helps me contribute to the leadership pool for the industry at large. I create new opportunities and challenges for leaders to grow.'

Ramesh Mangaleswaran says, 'Keep throwing challenges for the next level. As a leader, learn to let go of things and take on the next level of challenge. At McKinsey & Company, it is built into the system to keep growing and take on something that you didn't do before.'

A key watch out here is for leaders not to set unrealistic expectations and let their teams fend for themselves, which can be quite overwhelming and unproductive. If leaders do not mentor and coach their teams and provide the necessary psychological safety along with resources, the teams will struggle to meet expectations. Instead of harnessing their potential, they will feel more stressed and burnt out.

There are many leaders who demonstrate 'unsupportive accountability'. Sylvia Melena, author of *Supportive Accountability—How to Inspire People and Improve Performance*,[60] characterizes this style as being too demanding, harsh and intimidating. These leaders may set high performance standards and raise the bar but do not provide the resources and support needed to achieve the goals.

This is the leader who says, 'I don't care how you do it. Just get it done.' While this may spur a few employees to rise to the challenge and push the envelope, it does not serve to create the right kind of soil in which all people can thrive.

Leaders need to inspire through supportive accountability. When people do not meet the high targets set for them, the supportive leader does not blame or punish. The leader understands the reasons for non-performance and, together with the team, ensures that they are better prepared to meet it the next time.

Vikas Srivastava believes there should be a balance between person and policy. Working on personal transformation has to be balanced with accountability. He practices management by walking around, building deep connections and finding holistic solutions to problems.

One example of a leader who did this very well is Microsoft's Satya Nadella. When Nadella took over as the CEO of Microsoft in 2014, the company was facing declining revenues and loss of market share. Nadella created a bold vision, which included becoming a leader in cloud computing, a new area for Microsoft. He set the bar high and also inspired others by building a culture where empathy, diversity and open communication were valued. He also helped to create a growth mindset in the company where learning and experimentation were valued. 'A learn-it-all does better than the know-it-all,' Nadella said on a podcast with Jessi Hempel.

Shiv Shivakumar says, 'Leaders should inspire others by setting high standards, following the rigour and discipline and holding themselves accountable. Everyone has fears; they need emotional anchors to face their fears. Being a strong emotional anchor for your team can be inspiring.'

'Creating a bold vision and then empowering my team to achieve that vision is the best way to nurture my team,' says **Rajesh Jejurikar.**

Inspiring leaders strongly believe in continuous improvement to nurture themselves and see that as a means for others to nurture themselves. They are constantly looking around them across markets and across industries, actively seeking best practices that they can 'lift and shift' in their organization to enhance growth and productivity. They actively encourage this of their teams as well. As a result, the water table for creativity and innovation goes up, leading to new growth opportunities. This also has a positive impact on the team in becoming more entrepreneurial and enhancing their situational agility.

Motivate others for their growth

Leaders have always been motivators. Kings and generals have motivated scores of people to follow them and lay down their lives for them. Most leaders motivate their people to achieve results and perform better. They do this through a variety of influencing and motivational techniques.

Nurturing leaders motivate people to fulfil their potential. They engage with their people in a compelling way, helping them to become more self-aware and spurring them to action. Inspiring leaders understand that intrinsic motivation is necessary for personal growth and development, and they help people tap into their own motivators.

Anupriya Acharya often thinks about how to motivate the team. As a young leader, this was her chief concern. How to get people to feel motivated about their jobs and bring their best selves to work.

Navneet Saluja says, 'We try to create an environment that is non-threatening; it starts with how I conduct myself. We create an ecosystem where everyone can bring their true selves to work.'

Identify the different motivators

Daniel Pink's book *Drive* talks about how the traditional extrinsic motivation (Type X) using the 'carrot-and-stick' approach is now outdated and often ineffective in fostering true engagement and productivity.[61] Instead, Pink argues that intrinsic motivation (Type I), which is the drive to do things because they are inherently interesting, meaningful or enjoyable, is the key to sustained motivation and performance. Pink goes on to identify three core elements of intrinsic motivation, which he refers to as autonomy, mastery and purpose.

Autonomy

Autonomy is a basic human desire to direct our own lives. It emphasizes how people are more motivated when they have control over their work in terms of what they do, how they do it, when they do it and with whom they do it. Autonomy fosters a sense of ownership and accountability, increases engagement, creativity and job satisfaction.

Mastery

Mastery is the inherent urge to get better at something that matters. People are motivated by the desire to improve their skills and competencies and achieve a sense of progress in meaningful tasks. Mastery requires consistent effort, a lot of practice and the right level of challenge. Mastery leads to deeper engagement and a sense of accomplishment and fulfilment.

Purpose

Purpose is the desire to work towards something larger than ourselves. People want to feel that the work that they do on a daily basis has meaning and ultimately contributes to a greater cause. By connecting their tasks to a broader purpose, it inspires commitment and a sense of belonging. Purpose motivates people to go beyond self-interest and work toward shared goals.

Nurturing leaders listen for the motivators. They understand that different people are motivated by different things. Monetary incentives work with some people, recognition is needed by others, yet others are motivated by challenges that stimulate their thinking.

Nurturing leaders are invested in their teams and help them to find their drivers, their purpose and show them how this aligns with the larger organization purpose. They often invest their time and energy in working with their team members on their core values and larger purpose. They do this by asking powerful questions and by helping them navigate through the various choices. This motivates their team to lead happier and more fulfilling lives.

Hina Nagarajan says, 'I motivate my team and believe that they can achieve anything they want when they set their hearts and minds to it and are willing to work hard for it. When people identify their purpose, both personally and professionally, and then use work as a platform to shape their legacies, they are sure to succeed. This is the success mantra that I try to inculcate in each of my team members.' **Aditya Ghosh** adds, 'I try to play a catalytic role in helping people achieve their true potential. I understand what drives that person, what is their dream and how can I help them in that journey.'

Inspirational leaders nurture others by motivating them to be a better version of themselves. They are able to articulate a clear, compelling vision for the organization that connects with people's values and aspirations. In the process, they ensure that the individual's vision and values are aligned with that of the organization. They make sure everyone understands the 'why' behind the work, creating a strong sense of shared purpose. They are then able to effectively take others along on that journey.

Says **Manshul Nagpal, sales director at Mondelēz Asia,** who worked with Rajesh in Perfetti, 'Rajesh embodies every tenet of a great leader. He encourages you to put your best foot forward, to have courage, perseverance and commitment to one's success path. He has always inspired me to embrace risks/challenges and strive for growth every day.'

Use storytelling

Leaders are great storytellers and are able to evocatively communicate their vision in a powerful manner. Storytelling is different from telling stories, which is what gives storytelling a bad name. Leaders are not snake oil salespeople who spin a good yarn to make a quick buck. Storytelling is a way of weaving the communication in an interesting and compelling way as per the needs of the audience. Great leaders have always used stories to inspire. Barack Obama's 2008 presidential campaign often used stories. [62]The story of Ann Nixon Cooper, a 108-year-old woman, and that of the incident of 'Fired Up and Ready to Go' are classic examples of humanizing people and creating effective stories. Humans are wired for stories. As a facilitator, Nirupama has seen the power of stories over a framework. Using a story to illustrate and enliven a concept creates curiosity, interest and an aha moment for the audience.

Storytelling is a key aspect of inspiring and nurturing others. Insipid messages do not inspire. Inspiring leaders are generous with sharing their personal stories and the lessons that they have learnt from them. This enables their teams to avoid similar pitfalls and also gives them confidence to face any obstacles. The other aspect of storytelling is about evocatively communicating to the larger team the organization's vision and 'what's in it for them'. This leads to a seamless alignment between the personal and organizational vision, thereby significantly increasing the chances of success.

Nirupama inspires others by sharing her story in workshops and on platforms and raising the bar for what women can do. She has been invited to share her story in books and podcasts like the SheVolution stories of Inspiring Women by Kotak Life Insurance, the About Her podcast and the Unstoppable Women podcast, among others.

Alpana Titus uses storytelling to inspire others. 'I understand the context and then crystallize things for myself. I then simplify the narrative and tell the story to the team.'

In the study on the 'Role of Charismatic Leadership',[63] Jay Conger and Rabindra Kanungo's research examined charismatic leadership, identifying it as a behaviour-driven style that inspires enthusiasm and devotion. Charismatic leaders convey a powerful vision and demonstrate high confidence and strong personal conviction.

Rakesh Sharma adds, 'I nurture and inspire my team through my stories. These stories are not just about business; they are more about life. I make them more aware of themselves, help remove their anxiety and build their self-confidence to enable them to grow to their potential.'

Jagrut Kotecha believes sharing his stories with vulnerability helps him connect with and inspire his team. He says, 'I discuss non-work issues with them and actively share my stories with them.'

Charismatic leaders have a profound influence on their followers' emotions, inspiring high levels of motivation and loyalty. Their personal charisma can create a deep emotional connection, which often translates into enhanced performance and commitment.

Nirupama has designed and delivered several learning journeys and programmes on inspirational leadership for senior leaders and storytelling was a critical component of inspiration. However, many leaders lack this trait and struggle to master the skill of weaving a compelling narrative. Storytelling is a skill that can be learnt. Today, there are many workshops, books and videos that help leaders learn the art of storytelling to inspire.

Role model nurturing behaviours

'Being a role model is the most powerful form of education,' said John Wooden, the legendary American basketball coach.

One of the very important ways in which leaders inspire and nurture others is by role modelling key behaviours of Nurturing Leadership. These behaviours require the qualities of authenticity, compassion, resilience, perseverance, empathy, vulnerability and courage. Leaders need to walk the talk and demonstrate these behaviours visibly and consistently across their various interactions, which then inspires their team to follow suit. **Amrita Randhawa** says, 'As a leader, I need to act as a role model and need to have a standard for excellence for myself. Only then can I lead by example. People around us watch us quite carefully. When you cut corners and walk past standards, it gets noticed.'

Rajiv Rajgopal is a role model by being approachable and accessible and by being grounded. 'Leaders need to be relatable,' he emphasizes.

V. Anantha Nageswaran says, 'The best thing a leader can do is to set an example and let others observe and learn; teaching or preaching may not be effective and can even be counterproductive.'

Narmeen Khan believes she needs to walk the talk and be a role model for others. 'People observe leaders—how they behave, and what they say and do and take inspiration from there. I am mindful about how I behave during meetings.'

I, **Rajesh,** am passionate about health and holistic well-being. Over the years, I have motivated a few of my team members to take better care of their health by demonstrating genuine care for their well-being. I got two of my colleagues to quit smoking and I don't think I could have done this if I was not practising what I preached.

Rahul Chaudhary of Perfetti Van Melle who worked with Rajesh in Dhaka, says, 'Thanks to Rajesh for motivating and encouraging me to take fitness as a priority in life and showing me that every mile run is a step towards a stronger, more empowered self.'

Arundhati Bhattacharya likes to walk the talk and lead by example. She likes to share her learnings with others to inspire them.

Leaders can be role models in specific skills such as problem-solving, strategic thinking, influencing and public speaking, among others. As role models, leaders need to demonstrate certain nurturing behaviours that can help to nurture others. We look specifically at the behaviours intended to nurture and bring out the best in others.

Here are what we have identified as key behaviours and qualities that nurturing leaders demonstrate, which in turn inspire others to be more nurturing.

Authenticity

Authentic leadership is about bringing your whole self to your work and leading with your values, integrity and vulnerability. This then inspires others to be authentic and thereby nurture themselves. **Suresh Narayanan** stresses the importance of role modelling as a leader to inspire others. He says, 'Inspiring others is all about authenticity in action, having the right competence and expectations and compassion.'

Compassion

Compassion is about valuing others and making them feel cared for. In today's context, compassion for self and others is extremely important. Compassion starts with the self. Nurturing leaders are compassionate towards themselves and invest in self-care. They know that even the best-laid plans can come undone given the uncertainty all around us. This makes them be kind towards themselves. They also know that they have to take care of themselves so that they can take care of others. This then allows them to have the positive energy to nurture others.

In the study, 'The Role of Compassionate Leadership',[64] Richard Boyatzis and his colleagues examined how leaders' compassionate behaviours influence organizational culture, focusing on how leaders balance compassion with accountability. What they found was that leaders who model compassion create an organizational culture that values people, leading to increased motivation and loyalty. Employees in these environments report feeling more connected to their work and colleagues, which improves teamwork and morale. Compassionate role modelling by leaders creates a culture of care and mutual support, helping organizations retain talented employees and foster greater commitment.

Resilience and perseverance

There is so much uncertainty all around us that we will very often need plans B, C and D. The macro environment is fraught with risks and uncertainty. Wars have become more commonplace, natural calamities are on the rise and predicting the future has never been harder. In this context, it is important for the leaders to build resilience and perseverance in themselves and their teams. This helps them to navigate through turbulent times with minimum levels of stress.

Empathy

We have spoken at length about empathy in other sections of the book, but it continues to remain a key component of Nurturing Leadership behaviours. Inspiring leaders demonstrate high levels of emotional intelligence and empathy, which then get cascaded in the organization.

A study on 'Impact of Empathetic Leadership on Organizational Culture'[65] on emotional intelligence found that leaders who practice empathy create positive organizational climates. Empathetic leaders help cultivate an organizational culture where employees feel understood and valued, which leads to higher engagement, job satisfaction and team cohesion. When leaders model empathy, employees are more likely to replicate it in their interactions, leading to better collaboration and reduced conflicts. This study shows that role modelling empathy and emotional intelligence can improve organizational culture by promoting a supportive and inclusive environment.

Vulnerability

Inspiring leaders show vulnerability by admitting when they don't have all the answers or when they need help. This level of authenticity humanizes the leader and fosters deeper connections with employees. By being vulnerable, leaders create and encourage a culture where employees feel comfortable expressing their own fears and challenges and seeking support, thereby enabling personal and professional growth.

Courage

Courageous leadership is all about making bold, principled decisions and taking action in the face of fear, uncertainty or adversity, keeping in mind the well-being and growth of others. By demonstrating courage, leaders inspire, motivate and nurture those around them, fostering a culture of resilience, trust and continuous development.

Courage is also about making tough decisions with compassion. Courageous leaders stand up for what is right; they stand by their team and create an environment that fosters experimenting and learning. This can have a profound impact in terms of nurturing their team and encouraging them to step out of their comfort zone and go that extra mile.

In summary, role modelling Nurturing Leadership behaviours can be an extremely powerful way for leaders to inspire and nurture others. This can have a profound and lasting impact on the organization. In 'The Ripple Effect of Positive Role Modeling',[66] Barbara Fredrickson's research on positive emotions highlights the 'broaden-and-build' theory, where positive behaviours and emotions, such as support and empathy, expand people's capacity to build resources, resilience, and relationships. This showed that leaders who model positive behaviours set off a 'ripple effect', where others in the organization adopt similar nurturing behaviours, creating a culture that is more resilient, adaptive and collaborative. Positive role modelling by leaders has a cumulative impact, enhancing organizational culture by encouraging nurturing behaviours across teams and levels.

Magdalena Nowicka Mook sums it up well: 'Role modelling for leaders is very important. A leader has to balance the needs of the organization with genuine concern and interest for the individual.'

Leadership is a privilege that is bestowed upon a select few, and it needs to be used wisely to create the maximum impact on both business and people. **Radhika Gupta** says, 'Leadership is something that you learn by doing. Life is the greatest school of leadership. It is a privilege to be able to influence the lives of others. Leadership is leading by example.' **Pankajam Sridevi** echoes the sentiment:

'Leadership is not just a responsibility but a privilege. Every day I think about how I make myself worthy of being their leader. I want my people to bring their soul to work. They must come for the sake of the pride, respect and inspiration that they get from leaders.'

Inspiring leaders would do well to keep the chain going and pay it forward so that over time Nurturing Leadership behaviours become the norm across organizations. **Pramath Sinha** says, 'I wouldn't have reached where I have without the support and nurturing of the leaders whom I have worked with. I want to pay it forward. My work allows me to inspire and nurture a lot of young people. I get pride in the fact that they have gone on to be successful. All my success has come from making others successful.'

Practical tips for inspiring and nurturing others

1. **Operate one level up:** Take on a couple of projects that allow you to operate at a level higher than the one you aspire to. Do that with your team as well by giving them one or two strategic projects. This way, the overall bar is raised.
2. **Foster a growth mindset:** Create rituals and norms that encourage a growth mindset in the team. Always ask, 'How can this be done?' as opposed to, 'Can this be done?'
3. **Help create individual purpose:** Invest your time and energy in helping each team member create their purpose and then help align that to the organization purpose.
4. **Recognize and openly acknowledge nurturing behaviours:** Even as you role model Nurturing Leadership behaviours, appreciate and acknowledge

when team members demonstrate any of the behaviours.
5. **Show compassion to yourself and others:** Be kind to yourself and others; make others feel valued. Appreciate yourself more often than you criticize yourself. Recognize others' contributions for their efforts and not just the end results.

INSPIRE TO GROW

- OPERATE ONE LEVEL UP

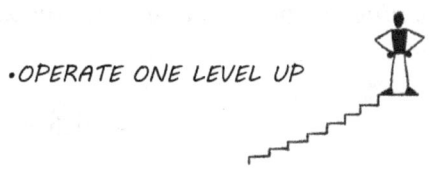

- FOSTER GROWTH MINDSET

- HELP CREATE INDIVIDUAL PURPOSE

- RECOGNISE NURTURING BEHAVIOURS

- SHOW COMPASSION TO SELF & OTHERS

11

Listen Actively

'Lead by listening. To be a good leader, you have to be a great listener.'

—Richard Branson

Listening to someone is like offering them water to quench their thirst. Humans are thirsty for attention, acknowledgement and understanding. Listening provides that, like a cool, nurturing balm to the human soul. Listening organizations are learning organizations where people thrive. Active listening is needed at all stages of nurturing, beginning with the hiring interview when listening helps select the right candidate. Listening is an important part of coaching and works in tandem with powerful questioning. We believe that listening is a crucial nurturing behaviour, which is the foundation for most of the other behaviours as well.

Most people think of listening as an activity and a passive one at that. Listening is different from hearing. We hear noise; we hear distant sounds; we hear people talking—we hear multiple sounds on a daily basis. Hearing is an involuntary, sensory process of perceiving sounds.

Listening is a skill. It is a psychological process. It is hearing with thoughtful attention. It is the process of making sense of the information we receive. In the context of conversations, it provides both information and involvement. One of the most impactful and eye-opening sessions in the leadership development workshops that Nirupama facilitates has been the segment on listening.

If we don't listen well, it can lead to wrong decisions, misunderstandings, misinterpretations and incorrect actions. The Ladder of Inference model by Peter Senge and Chris Argyris, used in the context of conversations shows how this simple act is a seven-step process.[67]

1. **Observation:** We start by observing a situation or event. However, we cannot observe everything, so we select and focus on certain aspects based on our personal biases, experiences and beliefs. We don't listen fully or deeply.
2. **Selecting data:** From the information we observe, we filter and select certain data points that seem relevant to us. This filtering process is influenced by our personal preferences and existing mental models.
3. **Adding meaning:** Once we have selected the data, we ascribe meaning to it based on our beliefs and assumptions. We interpret the data through the lens of our existing knowledge and past experiences.
4. **Making assumptions:** Next, we make assumptions based on the meaning we have assigned to the selected data. These assumptions may be unconscious and are often influenced by our biases and preconceived notions.
5. **Drawing conclusions:** Based on our assumptions, we draw conclusions about the situation. These

conclusions may be incomplete or distorted due to the limited data we have considered, as well as the biases and assumptions we hold.
6. **Forming beliefs:** We adopt beliefs based upon the conclusions we have drawn from our current situation, which may be stronger if also based on conclusions drawn from past experience. Our beliefs are further reinforced and applied in similar future situations.
7. **Taking action:** Lastly, we take action based on our conclusions. Our actions are driven by our beliefs and assumptions, which may not accurately match the reality of the situation. This can lead to misunderstandings, conflicts, and ineffective decision-making.

The whole process takes a few seconds, but the consequences of an incorrect assumption or decision can take much longer to repair.

Imagine a scenario in which a team member tells a leader, 'I haven't been able to complete the presentation. I'm facing a problem.'

The leader, based on past experience or biases, can interpret the situation to mean, *My team member is incompetent.*

The assumption is that the team member doesn't know how to carry out a simple activity and is creating problems.

The conclusion the leader can draw is that the team member will not be able to do justice to the presentation.

It could reinforce the belief *I have to do everything here myself!*

The leader may say, in an irritated tone, 'Send it to me. I will take a look.'

This may not solve the problem; in fact, it will create additional work for the leader and also leave the team member feeling disempowered.

We have observed such instances multiple times.

The underrated skill of listening has not been traditionally associated with leaders. Leaders were those who spoke, gave orders, made bold decisions and led the way. Communication was supposed to be one way, and good employees did not question the leader. Leaders did listen for information, facts and reasons to make better decisions. They were forced to listen to customers for their feedback and needs so that they could make better products and services. They rarely listened to nurture and grow others.

However, there has been a shift in the past few years. Listening has emerged as a key leadership skill. In Dr Steven Covey's bestselling book, *The Seven Habits of Highly Effective People*,[68] first published in 1989, Habit 5 is 'Seek First to Understand, Then to be Understood.' The only way to do that is through *listening*.

Sylvia Ann Hewlett's 2014 book, *Executive Presence*, was based on research conducted by her in 2012. She carried out a similar study in 2022 to understand whether the traits associated with the three pillars of Presence—Gravitas, Communication and Appearance—had changed. One of the new traits of a leader under the aspect of Communication was the 'Listen to Learn' orientation. This seemed to have replaced the trait of 'Forcefulness', which did not figure in the 2022 research findings.[69]

In his 2001 bestseller *Good to Great: Why Some Companies Make the Leap . . . and Others Don't*, Jim Collins stressed on the importance of listening as a leader: 'There's a huge difference between the opportunity to "have your say" and the opportunity to be heard. The good-to-great leaders understand this distinction, creating a culture wherein people had a tremendous opportunity to be heard and, ultimately, for the truth to be heard.'[70]

Listening helps in nurturing.

When leaders listen with attention, they help to unlock the potential of others.

In her 1999 book, *Time to Think: Listening to Ignite the Human Mind*, Nancy Kline described the transformative power of listening. 'Attention, the act of listening with palpable respect and fascination, is the key to a Thinking Environment. Listening of this calibre is enzymatic. When you are listening to someone, much of the quality of what you are hearing is your effect on them.'[71]

When people feel heard, they give their best; they think better; they come up with better ideas and they feel a sense of connection and belonging.

Leaders need to be good listeners. In 2019, an organization called Sideways 6 in the US asked for nominations for the best listening leaders. The list included leaders like Indra Nooyi of Pepsi, Satya Nadella of Microsoft, Steve Rowe of Marks & Spencer and Sundar Pichai of Google, among many others.[72]

In a 2015 interview with the *Wall Street Journal*, Satya Nadella shared his three simple rules of effective meetings, 'Listen more, talk less and be decisive when the time comes.'[73] Many of the leaders we spoke to agree that listening is important and it has many benefits. 'I strongly believe in deep listening; I have an open-door policy; I meet people across levels; it gives me a good insight into the psyche of the organization,' says **N.P. Singh, ex-MD and CEO, Sony Pictures Network India.**

Madhav Kalyan believes that listening is important to grow and develop the people. 'I listen and ask the right kind of questions. Personal conversations help people think about their career and get out of their comfort zone.' 'As a leader, I have realized that most of the time what your team truly needs is to be heard. Offering them your time and listening with empathy create space for emotional expressions, which often matters more than logic or behaviour. Empathy isn't just kindness; it is strategic enabler of trust and alignment,' says **Sivakumar Sundaram**.

Debjani Ghosh believes that listening is an important aspect of nurturing others. She says, 'Employees need to feel respected. Active listening and creating the right environment for everyone in the hierarchy to openly share their views can go a long way to enable this.'

However, listening is not an easy skill to practice. There are many barriers that come in the way of focused listening. Some of these barriers are external and others are internal to the leader.

Time to listen

Leaders have to juggle a thousand tasks. In today's hyper-digital world, they could easily be jumping from one online meeting to another. They have a packed calendar, and even with an assistant to manage it, there is little time for conversations that require deep listening.

Yet, giving your time is the best way to nurture others, says **Vinita Bali**.

Space to listen

Even if a leader makes the time to listen, it is not easy to get into the calm mind space required for deep listening.

There is too much noise in the world outside, too many preoccupations and distractions that can keep the leader from truly listening. The demands of multiple stakeholders, multiple social media channels and multiple business issues keep the CEO from giving complete attention in the present moment.

While leaders may not have listening as a goal, it is important to create time for this in the calendar. Some leaders like to keep a separate day and time. Some like to weave it into their everyday schedule. Do what works for you, but set this time aside and keep it sacrosanct. **Sandeep Sangwan** says, 'I have become better at listening and taking in diverse opinions. It also gives confidence to the team that the leader is open to new ideas. We have "listening lounges", where seven to eight members from the organization are picked at random and one member of the leadership team will meet with them and have a chat around any topic—typically picked up from organization survey topics. Each member of the leadership team does this once a quarter.'

Many leaders have a 'walk the talk' practice. **Nisaba Godrej** shares that she often takes a walk with people, focusing on asking questions rather than providing answers. People need to feel that you are listening to them, not just one person but many people across the board. **Sandeep Kataria** says, 'Whenever I travel to a city, I try to go for a walk with my colleagues and learn about the city from them. This helps me build connections and also get to know the city more intimately.' **Sathya Sriram** also combines walking time with conversation time. This also helps to increase the circulation and gives energy for conversations.

Mindset to listen

Listening requires a pause and a shift to a different mindset. 'Listening requires humility,' says **Suresh Narayanan**. It is about shifting the attention to another human being with an intent to understand and connect to them. Listening as nurturing is not about achieving a target or fulfilling tasks. Leaders who are in the doing mode need to switch to a being mode.

Ayushi Gudwani believes that she has learnt a lot just through deep listening combined with humility. Listening in this way not only connects to another but also nurtures the self.

Our mindset is impacted by the biases and beliefs that we hold, which become listening screens. Just like real screens, listening screens or assumptions prevent us from seeing clearly. It colours the quality of our listening.

Here are some common screens. They sound like factual statements inside our minds but are actually on-the-spot judgements and assumptions.

This is impossible.
I already know this.
I don't believe this.
There they go again.
They are blaming me.
There are so _____ (fill in with an adjective of your choice).

As human beings, we cannot avoid screens. Even if we clear one screen, a new one can easily pop up.

The best way to deal with these screens is to acknowledge them and become aware of them. Leaders cannot afford to be biased in their listening since it not only impacts their relationships with their team but also affects their ability to make good decisions.

If employees sense that the leader is biased or judgemental, it will affect the quality of their disclosure and trust levels across the board.

Suparna Mitra believes the leader needs to create psychological safety so that people can open up and talk about both their personal and professional lives. Many of these conversations may not have an agenda.

We believe that even if leaders have a listening mindset and create the time and space, they still can benefit from listening skills. While active listening, or listening with attention, is good enough to get information to make decisions, listening to nurture is an advanced form of listening.

Leadership experts Jack Zenger and Joseph Folkman outlined six levels of listening.[74] To become a better listener, put these steps into practice:

Level 1: You create a safe environment where pretty much anything can be discussed.

Level 2: You put away distractions like phones and laptops, and you make appropriate eye contact with the other person.

Level 3: You try to understand the main focus of what the other person is saying.

Level 4: You pay attention to non-verbal cues, such as body language, facial expressions or tone of voice.

Level 5: You understand the emotions and feelings of the other person, and you acknowledge them.

Level 6: You ask good questions that are designed to let the other person see a new perspective or challenge an assumption that they might have.

Listening with empathy

In an interview with Dave Rubenstein, Microsoft CEO Satya Nadella said, 'Empathy is an existential priority for a business. There is no way our innovation to meet unmet, unarticulated needs of customers is going to come about if we don't listen, not just to the words but go deep to understand what the needs are behind them.'[75]

Empathy is a critical aspect of 'Design Thinking', which starts with the first step of 'Empathize' before going on to 'Define, Ideate, Prototype and Test.'

Empathy is now recognized as a key quality for leaders. **Anusha Shetty** says that the empathy quotient needs to be high for all leaders across genders.

We mentioned empathy as a critical quality for nurturing leaders, and listening is the behaviour that allows leaders to demonstrate empathy.

Melda Yasar Cebe says, 'People want to be heard. I listen to them with all my senses. I am then able to play their story back in a way that makes sense to them. I have always been approachable, and I am fully present in meetings and conversations.'

Mohit Anand feels that treating people with respect and as equals is important to have an empathetic connection.

A 2021 study published by Catalyst[76] titled 'The Power of Empathy in Times of Crisis and Beyond' showed that empathic leaders make a big difference to employees. Sixty-one per cent of people with highly empathic senior leaders report often or always being innovative at work compared to only 13 per cent of people with less empathic senior leaders. Seventy-six per cent of people with highly empathic senior leaders report often or always being engaged, compared to only 32 per cent of people with less empathic senior leaders. The study shows that increased senior leader-level empathy leads to a lower intent to leave the organization by employees.

In the words of **Poul Weihrauch, CEO of Mars,**

> Some things will continue to change significantly—the geopolitical situation, the technology landscape, workforce demographics, as well as the state of our planet. Other things will remain the same. Humans will continue to seek connection and meaning in their lives. Empathy will matter more than ever, especially in an increasingly polarized world.[77]

Most leaders struggle with the demonstration of empathy. A leader coached by Nirupama was shocked to find that some of her team members had comments related to her lack of empathy in the 360-degree feedback report. She felt that she deeply cared about her team members, yet her behaviour during meetings and conversations was not congruent.

Many leaders confuse empathy with sympathy. Daniel Goleman defines three types of empathy in his book, *Focus: The Hidden Driver of Excellence.*[78]

Cognitive empathy: The ability to understand another's perspective.

Emotional empathy: The ability to physically feel what another person feels.

Empathic concern: The ability to sense what another needs from you.

All three levels of empathy require deep listening. It is impossible to be empathetic without giving your undivided attention to the speaker. It requires a whole-bodied presence that includes the first five levels of listening. 'Empathy fuels connection,' says Brené Brown, author of the book *Dare to Lead* and a leading speaker and researcher.

Speakers pick up empathy through the body language, facial expression, eye contact and energy of the listener. Then there is the quality of the acknowledgment or the response.

Imagine a team member is telling you *I feel overwhelmed. I am having a hard time. There is too much going on.*

What would you say?
Everyone is overwhelmed these days.
It is okay. You will feel better soon.
Would you like to go for therapy or take some time off?
I can send you for training on time management.
When I feel overwhelmed, I usually meditate for twenty minutes.

If you picked any of the above, then you are not being empathetic. While these statements are not wrong or show the manager to be callous and unfeeling, they do not demonstrate genuine empathy.

I, **Nirupama,** have done many sessions on Empathy as a part of leadership development initiatives. Like self-awareness, most people believe that they are empathetic but they are unable to demonstrate it during a simple role play.

Most people are quick to give a solution or offer advice. They mean well and are trying to help. But in most cases, the other person only wants to be heard and understood, not solved like an annoying problem.

An empathetic response can just be, 'Yes, it can be overwhelming with all that is going on' or 'I am sorry to hear that you are going through a hard time.'

Then give space for the speaker to share more by asking an open question. This enables a deeper conversation and connection. Try to have conversations with people beyond work. Ask about their families and homes out of genuine care. **Alpana Titus** believes that this is critical. 'You have to first connect with people with their hearts, then their minds. People don't care how much you know until they know how much you care. Be authentic and show people that you care.' **Retired Vice Admiral Anil Kumar Chawla** goes on to add, 'When we were in the seas, I used to meet one person per day on the ship for half an hour and listen to them share stories about their life and any other issues that they might have.'

Leaders can leverage effective listening to enable collaboration across functions and give an opportunity to people to work together to solve organizational issues. This leads to greater empathy and provides an opportunity to hear different perspectives. **Amit Syngle** has seen the effects of an organization-wide initiative to improve collaboration. The pillars of this collaboration initiative are Responsible, Caring, Empathetic and Affiliation (RCEA).

Listening as a skill can be learnt and sharpened. **Arnab Banerjee** shared that the coach training has helped him become a better listener. I, **Rajesh,** also benefited from enhancing my listening skills through my coaching practice. This was very helpful while listening to and mentoring my team.

Best practices on effective listening

1. **Create space and time:** It is important to create the right space—both physically and metaphorically—to enable effective listening. Set aside time where you don't have any distractions.

2. **Learn to listen:** Effective listening can be learnt. Listen with all your senses. Maintain eye contact while speaking to another person. Learn from those who listen well.
3. **Avoid biases and assumptions:** Leave aside your biases, assumptions and beliefs while listening. Listen with an open mind without judging.
4. **Acknowledge feelings while listening:** Empathize by connecting to the feelings of the other person. Saying this out loud lets the other person know that they have not only been heard but understood. Statements such as *I hear that you are feeling frustrated by the situation* and *It must be worrying to deal with this uncertainty* can let the speaker know that you are listening to facts and feelings.

LISTEN ACTIVELY

- CREATE SPACE AND TIME

- LEARN TO LISTEN

- AVOID BIASED ASSUMPTIONS

- ACKNOWLEDGE FEELINGS WHILE LISTENING

12

Empower to Thrive

'Leaders become great not because of their power but because of their ability to empower others.'

—John C. Maxwell

My manager micromanages me every single day.

In my organization, we are not encouraged to ask questions; we are just told to carry out tasks.

I don't get to learn in my job because I don't get the freedom to ideate, experiment and try out new things.

We often hear these comments across organizations. Empowering others as a core aspect of the organization culture is still evolving in many organizations.

As someone famously said, 'A leader's job is not to do the work for others; it's to help others figure out how to do it themselves so that they get things done and then succeed beyond what they thought was possible.'

Empowering their teams is one of the key traits of successful and nurturing leaders. So what is empowerment? It is about giving authority, freedom and responsibility to team members to make decisions and take action within their designated roles. It is also about providing them with the right training and resources required to perform the job. An empowered team is one where the knowledge, experience and motivation that already exist within the team are fully leveraged. The team is then able to perform at a higher level as a well-coordinated unit.

Why is it important?

Empowering your teams means that you are able to effectively delegate work to your team. This helps them learn faster and operate at a higher level. This also frees up the leader's time to do higher-order work. As a result, the water table of the entire team goes up. This will ultimately lead to a steeper learning curve and faster career growth.

Empowering allows leaders to spend more time on the balcony. Ronald Heifetz and Marty Linsky coined the phrase 'Move from the dance floor to the balcony' as a part of their research for their book *Adaptive Leadership*. The dance floor is in the domain of action and day-to-day tasks, whereas the balcony is the place from where you can get a good overview and a bigger picture of the actions. Leaders who spend more time on the dance floor can end up micromanaging and getting stuck in day-to-day operational issues. This gives the illusion of action but without progress.

Leaders need to spend more time on strategic issues and big-picture thinking by empowering others to take charge of the dance floor. Leaders also need to have a big-picture view of their own career and purpose. Leaders who see their role as developing the next line of leaders or focus on the next learning and growth for their own career are less insecure about their own future. The fear of redundancy does not then prevent them from empowering others.

Ramesh Mangaleswaran says, 'The most challenging thing for leaders is to let go. There is a huge sense of insecurity in leaders. If you don't know the next mountain ahead of you, letting go is a challenge. Can leaders give up 30 per cent of what they are doing and take in 30 per cent of new? If not, they will block others.'

Naveen Munjal says, 'In many ways, the balance of structure and spontaneity reflects how I lead. I believe in empowering my team to take decisions independently, even if things don't always go as planned. What matters is that those decisions are made with the right intent and the best information available at the time.'

Lt Gen. Anil Kumar Bhatt (retd) says, 'We all align on the vision and the big picture. I then delegate the tasks to my team; this is directly linked to the confidence I have in myself and my team. There is no pressure on targets. We all work together to find solutions rather than blame each other.'

Empowering energizes and motivates the team, as they feel valued and respected. This also drives them to perform better at their jobs, and the overall happiness level in the team goes up.

Empowerment boosts creativity in individuals and in the team, as people become more open to trying out new ideas without any fear of failure.

Empowerment ultimately leads to higher productivity, enriched culture and lower attrition.

Nurturing leaders empower others to grow and live their full potential. **Govind Iyer, board director of Infosys,** says, 'My purpose is to enable every person to be a better version of themselves. Nurturing others requires having a vision and building capacity at all levels, which will lead to the desired outcomes. At Egon Zender, we did a board effectiveness study on how to create better boards; we then built capability in each board member. Today, I do capacity building mostly in the area of philanthropy.'

Barriers to empowering others

As we can see, there are some very clear benefits of empowering teams. Why is it then that some leaders still find this to be a challenge? There are a few things that come in the way of effective empowerment.

Fear of redundancy

Many leaders find it hard to let go. Some feel that it might lead to them becoming redundant over a period of time, especially if there are some really smart people in the team. They believe that if they trained and empowered their team members, their job would be at stake. This leads to holding on to knowledge and information and, ultimately, to a lack of trust. Insecure leaders who are short-sighted will not empower others to grow. These leaders also limit their own growth and opportunities.

Fear of failure

There are leaders who feel that empowering teams and delegating to them might not produce the best results at the expected quality. These are leaders who feel that the quality of results of the team is a reflection of their own credibility and stature and are often reluctant to risk compromising on that. *What if I empower my team and they fail?* is a thought that often preys on their mind.

Fear of delays

A mid-level leader once told me (Rajesh), during a coaching conversation, that he doesn't delegate because he feels his team might take too long to get the job done, and he would rather do it himself and be done with it quickly. We then had a conversation around it to understand the real reason for the lack of delegation, and that turned out to be the fear of failure. We also did the math on the time that it would take him to do the repetitive tasks of his team versus the time it would take for him to guide them on how they can do it by themselves. He is now a successful manager managing a highly empowered team.

In order to be effective at empowering their teams, it is important for leaders to flex their style to suit the needs of the team. Leaders need to be able to toggle between encouraging their teams to soar and yet providing them with a safety net.

Meenakshi Nevatia speaks about creating a high-support, high-challenge culture as a means of building empowered teams

Tarun Arora says, 'Organizations to create sustained success must leverage the power of its people. My role is to challenge the team, raise the bar and prepare them to take the next leap. As a leader, we need to give them direction, while giving them space and ownership through empowerment to get the best out of them. Equally important is to create the right environment where the team feels safe to take calculated risks and commits to the bold decisions that push their boundaries.'

Apurva Purohit says, 'I have worked a lot on empowering women by showcasing their strengths to them and making them believe in themselves.' **Aditya Sehgal** says, 'I ask people the right questions and let them discover their own solutions and learnings. I act as a "door opener", and open doors for people—literally and metaphorically.'

There are predominantly four ways in which leaders can effectively empower their teams. These are around building mutual trust, creating a safe space, effective delegation and giving timely feedback.

Building mutual trust

Trust is a key element of empowerment.

A 2022 study by Edelman[79] found that when employees felt trusted by their CEO, manager and co-workers, they in turn trusted them more. When employees felt less trusted, it also impacted their performance and productivity apart from the trust they had in the leadership.

A 2024 Deloitte study[80] found that companies where employees felt trusted outperformed their peers by 400 per cent and 79 per cent of employees who trust their company feel more motivated at work.

There needs to be mutual trust and respect within the team for leaders to be able to empower their teams to perform at their potential. Trust leads to effective communication within the team so that issues can be discussed and addressed appropriately. This leads to a feeling of achievement and positive energy all around. Many leaders believe that trust has to be earned by the team members but often they do not have the luxury of time. It is important to start from a place of trust with sufficient guard rails in terms of organizational systems, processes and culture.

Vineeta Singh says, 'It all starts with trust and belief. I empower my team to do things themselves. My direct reports are very different people—one size never fits all. I am constantly thinking about how to make them better at what they do. I give people a lot of responsibility and freedom. I have their back. I am also vulnerable with them. People like transparency and to be trusted. Honesty and vulnerability help me to get the best out of people.'

Nisaba Godrej says, 'Telling someone in my team that I don't agree with you, but I trust you, and it's your call can be very empowering.' **Radhika Piramal** says, ' I believe in trust, faith and fairness. I encourage people to bring their whole authentic self to work, and I engage with them in an open and transparent manner. This makes them feel empowered.'

Vijay Subramanian, MD, AMEA of Bacardi, believes that timely and transparent communication helps to build trust, which helps in both good times and bad times. It creates an environment where everyone is comfortable being themselves.

Creating a safe space

When was the last time you felt empowered? When was the last time you felt like you could speak up without fear of any repercussions? When was the last time you felt you were at your creative best at work? If you think back on these questions, a common thread that would emerge is that you would have operated in an environment where you felt safe and comfortable enough to voice your thoughts, share your concerns and just be yourself.

Creating a safe space and providing psychological safety is a key prerequisite for empowering teams. Starting in 2012, researchers at Google spent two years studying 250 attributes of their 180 teams to understand the recipe for a successful team.[81] This Project Aristotle team had already identified four key factors that created a successful team: a) dependability, b) structure and clarity, c) meaning and d) impact. However, they knew there was a component missing, which was psychological safety.

The term 'psychological safety' was coined by Harvard Business School professor Amy Edmondson in 1999.[82] Psychological safety is there when team members feel safe to take risks and be vulnerable in front of each other. This empowers them to contribute ideas, develop solutions and add value to the team.

Since then, the benefits of psychological safety in the workplace have been well established and documented. According to a 2023 McKinsey & Company survey,[83] an overwhelming 89 per cent of employee respondents said they believe that psychological safety in the workplace is essential.

The leader has the responsibility of creating this safe space in the team where team members feel empowered to speak up without fear of consequences and bring their best selves to work.

Anil Arjun believes that the role of the leader is to create a space where people feel empowered. He does this by adopting two very important mindsets. The egalitarian mindset allows him to value each person for the skills, energy and time they bring to work rather than positions and roles or even past work experience. The abundance mindset enables him to create a space that is more nurturing and focuses on the wide potential of imagination and opportunities rather than operating from insecurity and competition. He focuses on each individual's career path, which is unique to the person, rather than expecting them to conform to some organizational structure. This helps each employee to be their best creative self.

Alok Mittal says, 'I give my team the space to operate. I encourage them to aim for stretch goals and support them to achieve it. I also provide a safe environment by being authentic and vulnerable. Employees feel safe and comfortable with failure; they learn from their experience and then move on.' **Bharat Puri** talks about building a proneurial culture in the organization, which is a mix of professionalism, like an MNC, and the entrepreneurial spirit of a startup. This empowers the team and allows them to take risks and be creative.

Vineet Nayar says, 'It is important for leaders to have the right intention to grow others, give them a white canvas to experiment and allow them to fail and learn. Leaders need to help people discover themselves.' **Greet Boonen** is a big believer in empowering her teams. She says, 'I am able to easily spot and develop talent. I create a safe space for my team, where they can grow together with shared values in a non-hierarchical environment.'

Kaushik Mukherjee adds, 'My approach is to build a rapport with my team so that I can push them to get the best out of them. I encourage them to take risks. I help create an environment where there are opportunities for people to grow above and beyond.' **Magdalena Nowicka Mook** prefers that people come to her with a problem rather than a screw-up. She focuses on building a culture of trust, openness and approachability so that this can happen.

Puneet Chandok fully trusts his team and likes to give them space to experiment, learn and move on; he enables them to be themselves. **Santosh Iyer** adds, 'I give space to my team to perform. They become more involved, act more responsibly and communicate upfront.'

Anuradha Acharya feels that it is important to create an inclusive environment. She does this by creating safe spaces to talk about stress at work and mental health issues. 'We want to normalize some of these things that are taboo.' She organizes events in the workplace where employees can build mutual trust and feel a sense of belonging. This has to be done on a regular basis, not as tokenism on International Women's Day or other such markers.

Effective delegation

Effective delegation is about striking the right balance between giving your team enough space to work to the best of their ability while being there to support them in times of need to ensure that the desired outcome is achieved.

Anand Kripalu takes an 'eyes on-hands off' approach. He says, 'I delegate to the team, and I will intervene only if required, but I usually leave people to do their own thing. My job is to make the whole larger than the sum of the parts.'

While delegating, ensure that you check for the three Cs: Do they have the required **capability** and **clarity**, and are there periodic **checkpoints** in place?

Toshan Tamhane says 'I agree on priorities with my team, but I don't get into the plan. I want my team to come up with solutions and details, which makes them feel empowered. If people feel trusted, they come up with better ideas. That way, only the critical issues come to me. I also tell them not to make their problem my problem. Initially, people don't like that, but they later feel like they have the mandate to do more things.'

Vikas Chawla says, 'I hold myself back and let my team take things forward. I only step in when asked for help. This frees up my time for more strategic things.'

One of the key things about effective delegation is also creating a sense of accountability and having clear metrics to determine the success of the task at hand. **Mike Spanos** says, 'Like in the Marines, at Delta, we are all about empowering at the frontlines. We trained our people relentlessly and resourced them—training, tools and processes. It is important to hold people accountable within the guardrails of the organization but not micromanage them.'

Another key aspect is around the adaptability of the leader. The extent of delegation and the feedback mechanisms would depend on the nature and composition of the team. It would also depend on the context—the nature of the job, the culture of the country and so on. The Situational Leadership Model proposed by Paul Hersey and Ken Blanchard in 1996 talks about flexing the task and relationship leadership styles based on the skill and will of the team member. A one-size-fits-all approach may work for some, but others may not feel empowered. **Mohit Anand** says, 'It is very important for me to have the right team. I get to know their strengths and opportunities and align the vision with them. I then give them the space to achieve their goals and put them on the podium.'

It is also important for leaders to ensure that the appropriate resources are made available. This can be in the form of capability building, monetary support and providing access to resources both within and outside the organization. **Suresh Narayanan** says, 'I identify talent young, give them the boundaries of my expectations, empower them and let them soar. A leader needs to be that eagle that nudges the eaglet to the cliff so that it can learn to fly.'

Delegation need not be only for tasks that need to get done as routine. It is important to look at delegation as a way of building confidence and enhancing the talent pool.

Anant Goel says, 'I tell my team to spend 80 per cent on their core function, 20 per cent on other functions. This gives them a holistic view, creates empathy and helps solve each other's problems. I get my vertical heads to present in board meetings—this gives them pride while instilling a sense of accountability and responsibility.'

Vijay Subramaniam believes that flexing of the style is critical for leaders. 'I need to know when to be in the trench and when to sit on the bench.'

Varun Berry says, 'It is important for leaders to ensure that they help build functional capabilities for their team and provide them with the relevant resources to enable them to succeed.'

Deepak Iyer has this to say: 'I realized a while ago that one area that required organization-wide capability building was data and digital expertise. In order to learn in this domain, we went on learning tours to the Tech & Innovation centres of Microsoft, Google, Accenture and others. I then encouraged my team to take up one digital-related objective and work on it. They then cascaded similar objectives across the organization. Very soon, we realized that many of our colleagues started building digital literacy and implemented POCs across different functions. We now have a lot more data and digital expertise in the organization.'

Giving timely feedback

'Feedback is the breakfast of champions,' says Ken Blanchard, a leading management guru and co-creator of the Situational Leadership Model.[84]

Nurturing leaders let their team have a nourishing, healthy breakfast. Putting in place the appropriate feedback mechanisms to monitor progress is a key aspect of effective delegation. When team members know that there is someone who can give them both positive and constructive feedback, they feel empowered to learn. Leaders need to pull out the weeds and manage performance so that the organization flourishes.

During my executive presence sessions and coaching, I, **Nirupama,** have witnessed leaders being hungry for constructive feedback. They want to know how they can learn and improve. While they appreciated the positive feedback, they were waiting to get to know their blind spots and correct them.

The word feedback sometimes has negative connotations. Feedback becomes negative if it is not delivered with respect and care. Feedback can become disempowering. It is seen as a negative thing that can reduce the self-worth of a person and have an opposite effect. Author of *Radical Candor* Kim Scott uses the term obnoxious aggression to describe the behaviour of leaders who are unable to temper their harsh criticism.[85] Instead, they can **challenge directly** and **care personally** to practise 'radical candor'.

When leaders use appropriate, respectful language instead of humiliating or calling others names, it empowers people to bring the right energy to their work. One of the leaders coached by Nirupama has received poor feedback from the team during his 360 ratings. One of the recurrent comments in the report was about his abusive language and harsh words. The leader was surprised to learn this. He thought that giving them feedback in a harsh, direct way would provoke them to change behaviour. Instead, people became too scared to be open and transparent about their progress and mistakes.

When feedback is given without care, the receivers become defensive or argumentative. It is an affront to their self-esteem and self-confidence. Many people go into the fight-or-flight response to poorly delivered feedback.

Sucheta Govil uses her intuition to quickly assess people based on their mindset, capability and stamina. She then spends time with them and empowers them to create the required impact. She does this by inspiring them and through periodic monitoring and feedback mechanisms.

Feedback is not just a routine or checkmark. **Mansi Tripathy** believes in both positive and constructive feedback as an empowering mechanism. 'I make the intention that I want this person to be really at the top. I think about how I want the other person to feel. This impacts my body language, my tone, my words and how I come across. I believe in thank yous and appreciation. If I appreciate people for what they have done with specific examples, I can make the person feel very special. This increases their self-worth and confidence.'

Mike Spanos says, 'You have to give them tough love. You give meaningful feedback. You give them moments of excellence. You also tell them where they are lacking and hold them accountable. Everyone who gets candid, meaningful feedback responds to it.' **Sunil D'souza** has periodic feedback sessions with his team which are open and allow two-way communication. He takes pride in helping team members uncover weaknesses. **Kirthiga Reddy** believes that the kindest thing you can do for people is to give them constructive feedback in byte sizes on a regular basis.

Nurturing leaders master the art of giving effective, positive and constructive feedback.

Here are a few tips to give effective constructive feedback:

1. Start with a positive intent for the growth and improvement of the receiver.

2. Separate the behaviour or issue from the person—mention the objective behaviour with facts and observations rather than make a judgement.
3. Mention the impact of the behaviour or action—this highlights the importance of making the change.
4. Make it a two-way process, listen to the other person and invite dialogue.

Leaders are communicating constantly not just by their words but also by their actions. What is unsaid and not acted upon is also a message that goes out to the teams. When leaders ignore mistakes, allow bad behaviours and don't penalize those who violate organizational values, the message goes out to the organization. The weeds start growing, and it will become difficult to pull them out later.

Aditya Ghosh summarizes it well: 'Power is at the centre of the word *empowerment*. It is about giving power to the team so that they can create impact and bring about sustainable change in their domain.'

Practical tips for empowering

1. **Build trust and create a safe space:** Trust begets trust. Start by trusting first. Trust your team and create a safe space for them to bring new ideas, try new things, learn fast and grow.
2. **Have a good feedback mechanism:** Have the right monitoring and feedback mechanisms to enable timely and effective communication within the teams. This will ensure that quick action can be taken in case of any issues. Create a culture of feedback.

3. **Flex your style:** Different strokes for different folks. Delegate to your team by using the style that works best for each individual. Use the Situational Leadership model to adapt your conversations.
4. **Provide the right resources:** People are empowered when they feel resourced. Teams need to have the right training, skilling, budgets and infrastructure. Providing resources within the budget and creating a nurturing environment help people perform at their best. Being frugal is good, but scarcity fuels insecurity and unhealthy competition. Spending mindfully on your people is a good investment, not an expense.
5. **Use empowering language:** Ensure that the language is positive and empowering. This is infectious and cascades down the organization. Don't curse. Don't abuse. Don't ridicule. Feeling seen and heard as an individual can be very empowering. Use people's names. Pronounce names correctly. Be genuinely interested in others.

EMPOWER TO THRIVE

- BUILD TRUST & CREATE A SAFE SPACE

- HAVE A GOOD FEEDBACK MECHANISM

- FLEX YOUR STYLE

- PROVIDE THE RIGHT RESOURCES

- USE EMPOWERING LANGUAGE

Section IV

Nurturing as a Practice

13

Who We Are Is How We Nurture

'Knowing yourself is the beginning of all wisdom.'

—Aristotle

All the leaders we spoke to felt strongly that nurturing the self and others was vital to being a leader, yet they did it in different ways. Some focused more on the physical aspects of nurturing the self; others were drawn to the mental aspects. Some leaders preferred a structured mentoring and coaching focus to grow their people; others felt that providing a nurturing environment that empowered the people was the best way to nurture them. Some were consciously nurturing the self and others; for some, it happened organically.

We identified the best practices and aspects of nurturing based on over 115 interviews that we conducted. We realized that there is no one fixed way to nurture one's self or others. When we examined the inputs along with our own research, we found that there are four main factors that accounted for the different styles and approaches to nurturing.

Personality traits

Personality plays an important role in determining how we prefer to nurture ourselves.

Most of us are familiar with the Myers–Briggs Type Indicator (MBTI), one of the oldest and most popular personality tests. The four dimensions of personality—extraversion–introversion, sensing–intuition, thinking–feeling and judging–perceiving-impact how we engage with the world in different ways. In fact, we organically gravitate towards certain ways of being and doing that are more natural for us.

Rajesh, who identifies as a high extrovert, prefers to connect and engage with people, build strong networks and have a more active social life. This nurtures his emotional domain and gives him the energy he needs. **Nirupama** is more of an introvert, drawing energy from within. She prefers to nurture the mental domain through reading, listening to podcasts and spending time by herself.

So Rajesh needs to be more intentional about finding time for reading or learning, and Nirupama needs to actively focus on enhancing connections to nurture her emotional domain. This is what we discovered when we took the Nurturing Quotient Assessment to understand our own NQ.

While engaging with others may be a natural style for leaders who identify as extroverts, nurturing requires a steady, quiet focus, which comes with an introverted style. Introverts can benefit from picking up the motivational techniques and engaging storytelling style of the extroverts to inspire others. Extroverted leaders, who are seen as role models, can be charismatic and flamboyant, but may not have the inclination for deeper coaching conversations and one-on-one connections.

Our personality also determines the approach we take towards nurturing activities. Those who are judging are more structured, data-driven and linear in their approach. Those who are perceiving are flexible, open and adaptable.

Judging personalities tend to be more disciplined about following routines and structures. Many leaders we spoke to kept aside a specific time for certain activities such as physical exercise, reading and socializing. Some tracked their activities on a spreadsheet and checked off completed items. Others were more fluid, preferring to adapt to the circumstances.

A perceiving leader says that 'It doesn't matter when I exercise as long as I get 10,000 steps done in a day.' A judging leader feels that 'It is best that I exercise for thirty minutes between 7 a.m. and 7.30 a.m. every weekday.'

A judging leader keeps a target of the number of mentoring or coaching sessions she will have with her team and sets aside a separate time to conduct these conversations. A perceiving leader chooses to spend time with his team for development conversations as and when the need arises. He may sometimes do it on the go, during a shared cab ride or over lunch.

Another commonly used personality profiling test, the dominance, influence, steadiness and conscientiousness (DISC), can also show how our behavioural preferences impact both the desire and ability to nurture others.[86]

A strong **D**, or **dominant**, style is usually a direct, commanding and bold problem-solver. Such leaders will provide stretch targets and raise the bar for their team. They are good at providing direction and guiding the team towards completion. Dominant leaders use competition as a way to bring out the best in others. On the flip side, these leaders are often impatient and poor listeners and cannot empathize with those who do not have a similar drive, level of confidence and result-oriented approach. They will provide feedback in a direct, abrupt manner.

The I stands for **influence**. The influencer is a people-oriented personality who likes to build relationships and connect with people. They are open, build rapport easily and like to engage in communication, especially to inspire and engage. A leader who is high on influence will nurture well by empowering others and offering space for people to grow. However, they may not provide constructive feedback when required, out of a desire to preserve the relationship. Their approach will be more organic than organized. They may believe that their outgoing, optimistic personality will serve to motivate people instead of taking specific intentional actions for developing them.

The S is for **steadiness**, a personality that focuses on collaboration, stability and support. The steadiness trait allows for nurturing others through empathetic listening, patience and a genuine concern for others' growth. S-type leaders can be great coaches and mentors who are truly invested in their people, who will take the time to grow their capabilities. However, the S-type leader prefers to avoid conflicts and will prioritize status quo over change. This can come in the way of direct communication with their people and taking a call on their people. An S-type leader coached by Nirupama did not challenge his team or provide them with opportunities outside their comfort zone. He believed he was doing this out of compassion and concern for his team members, but this also resulted in them not developing to their full potential.

The C, or **conscientious**, leader is accurate, process-oriented and quality-conscious. This leader will have a structured plan for the team, be meticulous in identifying and charting their team's capabilities and skills and set a high bar for the quality of work. These leaders are seen as dependable and trustworthy. Conscientious leaders sometimes lack the charisma and confidence needed to inspire people to go beyond boundaries. They may become focused on rules and regulations rather than the person's needs. People are often messy and unpredictable and the C leader prefers to avoid both.

Our personality provides direction and a path to nurture ourselves and others. A strength-based approach helps us to tap into the traits and skills we already possess. This helps conserve energy and allows for more ease.

While we need to be guided by what naturally energizes us, we may unwittingly neglect an important domain of energy that is necessary for holistic growth and development. Our personality is an asset, but it can also block us from our own greatness.

Values and beliefs

A few years ago, Nirupama coached a senior leader who stated that he wanted to improve his listening skills. While he was aware that he needed to work on this particular aspect, he failed to make consistent progress.

During the coaching session, he admitted to a belief: 'Listening to someone means obeying them. I can't do that as the leader of my team. I need to command them.' Even though he knew that listening was important, his belief acted as a limiting factor in nurturing others through listening.

Our values and beliefs guide our behaviours, which ultimately lead to the results we get.

If growth and nurturing are not values, they cannot be practised even though we know all the best practices.

It cannot become a sustainable practice even if we put in the effort.

Many of the leaders shared their values and beliefs, which impacted how they nurtured the self and others. **Mike Spanos** mentioned that he brought the Christian values of service and the belief around servant leadership to the workplace. He saw his role as being in service to the employees, the organization and the community.

Nisaba Godrej also shared that she grew up with the value of trusteeship—there is a strong sense of service to the larger community. **Santosh Iyer** believes trust begets trust. This enables him to be more empowering and share power with others. Joy is an important value for **Manu Anand**. He believes that you must enjoy your work and this impacts the energy you bring to your work and the team.

Ayushi Gudwani believes in commitment and care, which shows up in her approach to work and people.

Health was another important value for most of the leaders that we interviewed. Many of them admitted to being guided by this belief to institute practices and policies that also support employee health. **Anupriya Acharya** is one such leader who focused most of the staff welfare expenditure on enhancing employee health.

Values impact both the *why* and *how* of Nurturing Leadership.

Leaders who value discipline are more structured and adhere to the timetables that they create for the activities that nurture them. Those who value spontaneity and flexibility will shy away from putting in a routine or adhering to a structure. Leaders may sometimes struggle to prioritize values, which can create some dilemmas when it comes to nurturing the self and others.

Do I place my personal well-being over employee support?

How do I stay true to my value of authenticity while putting on a brave face in front of my employees, even when I'm feeling afraid?

Do I get results quickly by doing things myself, or do I allow the team to do it, even though it may take time?

How do I balance my need for results versus employee growth?

It is important to have clarity on our own values and live them consistently in the face of challenging times. While values are universally desirable, our beliefs around the values can be accelerators or brakes.

Internalized capitalism is a common phenomenon whereby people feel that their self-worth is directly tied to their productivity. This belief leads to a strong feeling of guilt if you are not constantly doing something you deem productive. Rest is seen as laziness, prioritizing work over well-being is seen as ideal and a constant feeling of inadequacy is a norm. Internalized capitalism does not allow for the time and space needed for nurturing self and others.

Another belief system that impacts our desire for nurturing others is that of *reciprocal altruism.* Reciprocal altruism leads to behaviours where we act to help others with the expectation that they will return the favour in the future. Reciprocal altruism offers several advantages in the workplace—it can lead to better collaboration, teamwork, information sharing, recognition, feedback and greater peer support. Reciprocal altruism may not always be desirable when it comes to nurturing others. Leaders who believe in this quid pro quo approach may invest in people selectively. High performers who promise better results may be favoured, given more coaching support and empowered to take on bigger projects over those team members who may be viewed as a risky investment. While this can lead to a strategic use of a leader's time, it may exclude those who really need nurturing and support.

All human beings have biases—both conscious and unconscious. These beliefs affect the choices we make about how and when to nurture the self and others. If a leader subscribes to the belief that 'you can't teach an old dog new tricks', she may not give time to the senior, older employees. On the flip side, a belief that equates wisdom with age will not allow for reverse mentoring or learning from younger people. Many leaders mentioned that they actually nurtured the mental domain by interacting with the younger employees and a more diverse workforce.

The halo and horn biases are cognitive biases that influence how we perceive and evaluate individuals based on a single positive or negative trait. A positive impression of an employee based on his punctuality may lead to an impression that he can also manage a large team independently. This may cloud a leader's judgement during delegation and empowering the team. On the flip side, a negative impression about an employee's communication style can lead to underestimating or misjudging his analytical skills, leading again to ineffective delegation.

Our beliefs and biases about ourselves impact the way we form and adhere to habits, especially when it comes to nurturing ourselves. James Clear, the author of *Atomic Habits*[87] talks about identity-based habits. If a leader strongly believes *I am not a meditator*, it will impact his ability to stick to a meditation practice. An identity of *I am a runner* will help participate in a marathon and spur a daily running habit.

A leader coached by Nirupama shared, 'I am not a reader.' This impacted his ability to read and acquire knowledge needed for his growth. Even though he tried to set aside time for daily reading, something would always come up and eat into the reading time. The leader had associated reading with being a nerd; he had been an athletic sports person at school. This identity of being sporty came in the way of his reading. Finally, he came up with a solution to acquire knowledge that leveraged his desired identity—he listened to podcasts and books on Audible while on a brisk walk or a jog. Identity traps are also a result of a personality trait that a person is deeply attached to.

Leaders need to get clarity on their values and beliefs as they put in practices to nurture themselves. Alignment with values is important for sustainability. Prioritization of values is important for effectiveness. At the same time, an awareness of our biases and beliefs can help to unlock inertia or the feeling of being stuck and free up more options to nurture ourselves.

Culture

Culture is a shared set of values that lead to norms and behaviours for a group. The environment has a significant impact on how we nurture ourselves. One realm of culture is that of the organization that we are a part of. Organizational culture is created as a result of the values and beliefs of the founder. These values are adopted by all employees of the organization and lead to commonly followed norms. These aspects of the culture impact how leaders are expected to nurture themselves and work with the teams.

The leaders from the armed forces we spoke to were influenced by the norms of discipline and structure that were critical in their institution. The focus on physical fitness and maintaining that fitness routine was a norm in their context. Global sports brand Nike is all about fitness and many of the employee benefits revolve around health and well-being to promote a culture of health and fitness.

Some of the leaders we spoke with mentioned that they had initiated and supported a fitness culture in their organization. **Anupriya Acharya** mentioned the PubFit initiative at Publicis based on five pillars of well-being and longevity. **Hemant Malik** initiated FuroFit, an initiative that motivated people to walk and participate in a fitness challenge.

Does the organization have a work hard-party hard culture where people are expected to work fourteen-hour days and party hard on Fridays?

This may not leave much time or energy for an early morning run or time for coaching and mentoring conversations. Salesforce, founded by Marc Benioff, believes in the concept of Ohana, the Hawaiian family culture that fosters a sense of community and well-being. This allows for nurturing the emotional and mental domain through a sense of belonging, connection and strong work relationships.

Google's 'Search Inside Yourself' programme was one of the first workshops offered by organizations to support mindfulness and reduce stress. Companies like Aetna, Target and General Mills are also investing in supporting their employees to nurture their mental and emotional domains.[88]

Many organizations that **Nirupama** has supported through coaching have a coaching culture where leaders are expected to use a coaching style to engage with employees. **Rajesh** initiated a coaching certification process for the top leaders during his tenure as MD at Perfetti Van Melle.

If organizations have a nurturing culture that brings out the best in their employees, then leaders who uphold that culture also have an added advantage in nurturing others.

We also saw that the culture of the country has some impact on how leaders nurture themselves and others. While most of the leaders we interviewed were of Indian origin, many had lived abroad and had been exposed to several cultures. **Vignesh Nandakumar,** who has worked across four countries, noticed that Europeans prioritized activities that were focused on physical health and well-being, while Americans, especially in the Midwest, made time for family and family gatherings. South Africans never missed the Braai, a leisurely weekend barbecue with friends and family.

European cultures do place a greater value on work–life balance. The average European work week is forty hours, though several leaders do work longer than that. Leaders who have lived and worked in Europe also spoke about the importance given to physical activities and the sanctity of time with the family over the weekends. This enables leaders to recharge and nurture themselves in a more holistic manner.

The Nordic countries have consistently ranked at the top of the list of happiest countries in the world. These cultures lay great emphasis on nurturing all aspects of the self. The Danish trend of *faellesspisning* or communal eating brings people together and fosters a sense of community. The concept of *samfundssind*—putting the concerns of society higher than personal interests—gives people a sense of purpose and connectedness. An interesting Finnish word is 'kalsari-kanni', which celebrates relaxation by oneself. The people of Iceland build resilience in a hard climate through a philosophy of *Petta Redast*, an optimistic view that things will work out while the Swedish people believe in *lagom*, balance and moderation. Cultures that promote nurturing through connection, community spirit, physical fitness and leisure do see a greater overall well being of the people.

In many Asian cultures, there is a value placed on longer working hours, more so in certain industries like management consulting, investment banking, startups, advertising and the media. This tendency to value and give more emphasis to working hours versus self-care and nurture works well in the short term but can lead to stress and burnout.

Another aspect of national culture shows up in the leadership styles that are favoured. Western cultures are characterized by a more egalitarian, democratic style. Many Eastern cultures have a more paternalistic style. While both styles of leadership can be people-oriented, the way the people are nurtured and groomed does differ.

Alpana Titus speaks about the cultural nuances that need to be kept in mind while giving feedback. Direct feedback is seen as confrontational and not accepted in certain cultures.

In his book, *No Rules Rules*,[89] Netflix founder and CEO, Reed Hastings, and Erin Myers discuss the importance of respecting national culture while implementing the Netflix practice of radical candour. While direct, immediate feedback may work well with the Dutch and Germans, it did not go down well with Eastern cultures like Japan and Singapore.

Many family- and promoter-led organizations in India have a benevolent and paternalistic leadership style where the leader inspires loyalty and adherence by virtue of the family culture, where the head of the family is revered and respected. Leaders in these organizations focus more on inspiring and mentoring rather than listening and coaching.

Another interesting aspect of culture is the home culture. Even within the national culture, there are subcultures. Each family has a different set of norms when it comes to eating habits, sleep time, leisure activities, emotional patterning and spiritual practices. If there is a habit of eating late and sleeping late in a family unit, it is difficult for one person to stand out and follow a different pattern. Certain families have a late dinner around 9.30 p.m. and wind down only past midnight. Nurturing the mental, emotional and spiritual domains is also influenced by the practices of our families.

Nirupama is an avid reader and recharges and learns through books since this was an accepted and natural habit in her family.

Rajesh's family has been very social with an emphasis on meeting for family gatherings and maintaining connections, and this way of nurturing himself emotionally comes naturally to Rajesh.

Anuradha Acharya feels that her organization attracts people who have a high focus on health, and this helps to build a culture where taking care of your health is the norm. But this is not possible if the family does not support some of the practices they advocate. Her organization extends testing and counselling to family members of employees as well since the home culture has a huge impact on our exercise, food and sleep habits.

Even though national and organizational culture have an impact, we see that CEOs have the power both to drive and influence the subculture in the entity they lead. Most leaders spoke with pride about the nurturing culture that they are building and the practices that they have institutionalized in the organization during their tenure.

Demographics

Demographic factors also impact how we nurture ourselves and others. While we did not specifically check for this aspect during our research, the conversations showed us that there are differences in how we approach aspects of nurturing self and others. The two most important aspects of demographics that impact nurturing self and others are **age and gender**. We did not notice any correlation with other factors like race, ethnicity or education.

As we worked on this book, we realized that we started focusing much more on our well-being and self-care in our forties as compared to the earlier years. In our twenties, we did not think about purpose or contribution. Our focus was on doing really well in our jobs and, a little later, focusing on the family and leisure activities. Our thirties as young parents were more child-centred. We also found that many older male leaders were avid golfers—a sport that nurtured them physically and emotionally. Women leaders were more intentional and deliberate about taking time out for themselves, especially if they had young children. There are more men who are smokers compared to women. Men smoke as a way of bonding and connection. This does pose greater health risks as well.

Life stage impacts lifestyle. Younger leaders approach health from a fitness and readiness for activity perspective. As we grow older, nurturing the physical aspect becomes a preventive or maintenance activity. More health issues can surface later after several years of hectic work. High blood pressure, hypertension and stress-related diseases kick in after middle age. We become more aware of emotional and mental health at this stage and try to be proactive about taking care of these. While all leaders do have a sense of purpose and responsibility, the spiritual aspects of contribution and faith become more important at a later stage.

Nirupama works extensively with women leaders in the corporate world and outside. Many women have to juggle domestic responsibilities along with work. While the women leaders we spoke to had reached a life stage where they could afford help and had a system of support, this is not the case for many others. Women do struggle to prioritize their time for self-sustenance, and many find it difficult to set boundaries. This leaves less time for intentional activities that nurture them. Social conditioning and traditional norms codify me-time for women as self-indulgent, something that comes at the cost of nurturing others, usually her immediate family. We see very few women leaders who are avid golfers—golf takes up more time. Women look for quick fixes and activities that can be bundled with others to maximize time.

On the day we were working on this chapter, Nirupama was a panellist for a discussion organized by the CII Indian Women's Network. The theme for this panel was 'Are women expected to have a more Nurturing Leadership style?' This led to an interesting discussion on how gender determined the degree as well as acceptability of a Nurturing Leadership style. While we all agreed that nurturing was a critical leadership skill and activity, we knew that conditioning impacted the way we viewed qualities of nurturing. Women employees were always given the responsibility of taking care of food and caring for unwell employees, while men were not seen as patient listeners.

Nurturing others is both a mindset and a skill. While women may be conditioned to be nurturers, the skills of mentoring, coaching, listening and empowering can be demonstrated by any leader. Both male and female leaders felt that listening with empathy, creating psychological safety and empowering others were key leadership traits. Women leaders were more intuitive when it came to sensing what others needed and adapted accordingly. Many male leaders spoke about sharing their knowledge and wisdom as a way of nurturing others through mentoring.

These factors of personality, values, culture and demographics explain why no two leaders have the same approach or the same set of practices to nurture self and others. The fundamentals and best practices need to be applied in ways that are aligned to the context.

14

Strike the Right Balance

'Balance is not something you find; it's something that you create.'

—Jana Kingsford

Do you remember the three leaders whose dilemmas we shared in Chapter 1?

These leaders were grappling with multiple forces that took a toll on their well-being. They were pulled by seemingly conflicting priorities that created stress and made nurturing others a difficult task.

Nurturing Leadership isn't something that comes easily and naturally to all. The uncertainties of the job, the pressure to deliver quick results and an intense work schedule make it difficult to find the time and mind space to nurture both self and others. Leaders have to work at it. Everyday. And not everyone gets it completely right all the time.

One of the key things that we observed from all our conversations with these leaders was that in order for them to be successful at nurturing themselves and others, they needed to manage polarities and paradoxes.

Rajeev Dubey puts it well: 'Leadership is about managing seemingly polarizing ideas at two ends of the spectrum. It is important for leaders to peg themselves at the right point in that spectrum, and this would very often be contextual.'

Uttam Digga believes that it is important to operate with balance and not go to extremes. This helps put boundaries and guardrails.

In order to understand this better, let us go back a few centuries to look at the concept of the yin and yang emanating from ancient Chinese philosophy. It symbolizes the dual nature of existence, where opposites coexist and complement each other. The yin-yang symbol, embodying balance and harmony, illustrates how seemingly contrary forces are interconnected. Yin, often associated with femininity, represents the receptive, cool and inward aspects of things. Yang, on the other hand, corresponds to masculinity, embodying warmth, action and outward movement. This eternal opposition and unity between yin and yang highlight the importance of balance in the natural world, suggesting that life thrives when opposites are in harmony.

The same can be applied to leadership as well. Effective leaders realize that traits that are seemingly opposite to each other can co-exist and complement each other. They are able to be comfortable with both ends of the spectrum, quickly adapt themselves to the situation and flex their style accordingly. They operate in a virtuous loop of continuous learning through the process of unlearning and relearning. By adopting the yin and yang philosophy, leaders can create and foster harmony in their leadership style, achieving both short-term effectiveness and long-term growth for their organization, their teams and themselves.

Based on the 115-plus conversations we had with leaders, we identified three primary polarities that need to be balanced for effective Nurturing Leadership.
Discipline *and* flexibility.
Self-orientation *and* others-orientation.
Ambition *and* compassion.

Discipline *and* flexibility

Vipul, the business leader from Eat Well, Inc., whose story we shared in Chapter 1, could not strike the right balance between discipline and flexibility. Without discipline, his hectic schedule and work responsibilities took precedence over self-nurturing and mentoring his team. Even though he knew that exercise and spending time with his family and teams were important, he was not able to do so. In his desire to adapt to ever-changing circumstances, he may have lost sight of his core values and priorities.

It is common for people to let go of many things that are important in favour of the urgent fire that they need to put out immediately. They see extreme discipline at one end and a total free-for-all at the other as the only available options.

Discipline without freedom is tyranny. Freedom without discipline is chaos.

Discipline is about having a routine, creating rituals and sticking to them. It is about structure and adhering to one's goals. Flexibility is about the willingness and the ability to adapt plans to changing circumstances.

Nurturing Leadership requires us to balance between discipline and flexibility. This can be done in the following ways.

Set broad objectives and specific plans

Setting clear objectives for nurturing the self and for nurturing others is important. We saw leaders even go to the extreme of having an Excel sheet to track their goals and monitor on a daily basis. Objectives are overall goals that connect to purpose. You might set the objective of running a marathon or enabling at least three people in your team to get to the next level. Objectives are overarching. In order to achieve objectives, we need to have specific plans. Objectives don't change on a daily basis. Plans can be modified. The plan to prepare for a marathon can include an exercise schedule, a diet chart and regular runs. Plans to enable three people can include weekly one-on-one meetings, supporting them through coaching and mentoring them on new projects.

Leaders need to be very disciplined about achieving their objectives and give some flexibility to change plans if required. Being stuck on plans without a larger objective in mind defeats the purpose. Having only broad objectives prevents consistent action.

Track the KPIs

What gets measured gets done. Setting objectives and plans is the first step. Like everything else in business, nurturing self and others requires the creation of certain key performance indicators (KPIs) and the periodic monitoring and tracking of them. Rajesh tracks his daily physical activities in an Excel file. He also used to track the coffee connections that he did with the larger team on a weekly basis. This helped him stay the course and strike the right balance.

One of the reasons people measure the steps taken to help them to keep to a walking schedule is because there is a clear measurable KPI that also acts as a motivator. Tracking progress allows you to see if you are meeting the broad objectives, even if you fall behind on a couple of shorter-term plans.

Insist, but innovate

Once you set objectives and track KPIs, it is important to have the courage and conviction to stick to them in the face of opposition. Leaders are insistent about the big important things in their lives.

Mark Randolph, the co-founder of Netflix, had shared that he would leave work every Tuesday at 5 p.m. no matter what, for a dinner date with his wife.[90] This ritual kept him sane and grounded and provided the nurturing that he needed to take back to his job. There was no compromise on this.

However, there could be times when circumstances are beyond your control. In these cases, it is important to be creative and ensure that you have a viable plan B.

For example, a sudden travel plan might come up, in which case make sure to pack your running shoes and go for a walk when you get a break. Or meditate while you are on a flight in case you miss your early morning meditation. Many leaders combine a couple of activities in an innovative way that allows them to meet their broad objectives.

Rajesh is extremely disciplined about his fitness routine. He once did a twenty-minute walk up and down the aisle while on a twenty-hour transatlantic flight to get in his minimum non-negotiable daily exercise. **Nirupama** follows a flexible approach to learning. She is often not able to read regularly for thirty minutes every night as per her plan. Instead, she uses the two to three hours of domestic flight time to catch up on her books.

Balancing discipline and flexibility is about staying committed to your principles and goals while remaining adaptable to the curveballs that life throws at you. This approach helps nurturing leaders to progress steadily with resilience and perseverance, no matter what the external circumstances.

Self-orientation *and* others-orientation

Nusrat, the head of Boyd's GCC in India, was struggling to find the balance between self and others-orientation. Her social conditioning and circumstances led her to focus more on the needs of others, and she ended up feeling guilty and frustrated whenever she couldn't do that. Our own values and orientations are often in conflict with each other for the precious twenty-four hours in a day.

This is a delicate balance that nurturing leaders need to maintain. We know of many leaders who like to nurture others and invest their time and energy in doing so, often at the cost of their own well-being. We also know of leaders who take very good care of themselves, often neglecting the needs of their team.

Self-orientation is about taking care of one's well-being, having the right values and having a larger purpose so that one can perform to one's potential. It is about having the right focus on personal growth. Whereas others-orientation is all about taking into consideration the needs of others as well as valuing their well-being. It is about building relationships, supporting the growth of others and displaying empathy and compassion. It is also about collaboration and contribution.

Too much of either can be detrimental—extreme focus on the self can make the leader appear egoistic, selfish and narcissistic. This kind of self-obsession can lead to the leader not being able to see beyond the self. Whereas heavy emphasis on serving others can be seen as a sign of self-neglect and over-dependency on others.

So how does one go about nurturing oneself and others with the right balance? There is no easy answer. To use an airplane announcement analogy, it is important for the adult to first wear the oxygen mask before they put it on the child. Similarly, it is important for the leader to embark on the journey of nurturing themselves so that they have the energy to effectively nurture others.

There are a few strategies that leaders can adopt to strike the right balance between self-orientation and others-orientation.

Seek feedback from others at work and outside

Leaders receive less direct feedback from others. Most people find a leader's power position working as a deterrent to offering timely, constructive feedback. Leaders may discover their blind spots much later through poor performance, rapid attrition or other such symptoms. At home, they may receive indirect feedback from family and friends who don't relate to them as busy CEOs.

It is important to get feedback from the key stakeholders at work and outside to figure out whether you are able to balance the self- and others-orientation. Disconnection, distance, a feeling of emptiness and poor health indicators are signs of a leader needing to have conversations and receive honest feedback.

A leader could enlist the help of a coach to seek feedback from key stakeholders and from family and friends to help in personal development.

Prioritize the non-negotiables

A leader will have many things to do on a daily basis, from doing the most mundane tasks to making the most strategic decisions to effectively mentoring their team. Time is at a premium, and so is energy. A leader has finite time and energy. Hence, it is important that leaders prioritize their work and identify what are non-negotiables. In order to be nurturing leaders, they need to prioritize their people's agenda and set aside time for growing their teams.

One way to do this is to create a demarcation between the 'must-dos' and the 'nice-to-dos' for a particular time period. At least twenty minutes of physical activity could be a non-negotiable must-do, while one hour of exercise daily could be a nice-to-do.

A monthly one-on-one meeting with direct reports can be a must-do for a leader, while an informal connect with peers can be a nice-to-do.

This list of non-negotiables can include activities that nurture self and nurture others. A quick glance at these non-negotiables will help you to see if there is a balance between the self- and others-orientation. While this can change depending upon the context, it is important to balance it over a longer period of time. A leader can take time off for caregiving duties for a sick parent and spend a month purely with an others-orientation while doing a minimum of the must-do activities for self-care. At other times, a critical project may involve a longer duration of work travel or long hours at work away from the family. It is important to find an internal alignment during these times and ensure that we do not experience resentment, guilt, inadequacy or frustration.

Setting up these non-negotiables allows you to make choices that are aligned with your values and needs.

Set clear boundaries

It is very easy for leaders to get sucked into supporting and nurturing others. Leaders must avoid this trap by setting boundaries. Your time and, more importantly, your energy is finite; use it wisely. Learn how to say no to others where there is a risk of compromising your own well-being. Be assertive while respecting the other person's views and emotions.

Some leaders are very proud of their 'always open door' policies. While this fosters approachability and openness, these leaders may struggle to get tasks done on time and without distraction. The hero mindset, with them needing to provide a solution to everyone and swooping in to solve problems, may prevent them from thinking strategically and solving complex issues.

The fear of offending someone or losing a connection may prevent us from setting boundaries at home and work. A leader shared that this was a challenge, particularly during the Covid-19 years, when he strongly identified with the role of provider and protector of his family, even more than usual. This led to distracted, unproductive meetings as his attention was on the needs of the people outside the 'office' room. He needed to put up a simple 'Do Not Disturb' sign on the door for important meetings.

Set aside both me-time and time for others as non-negotiables. Many leaders set aside some time to meet their team members formally or informally during the course of the week. This could be over a cup of coffee, lunch or even a post-lunch walk. Mark this out on your calendar and respect it.

Balancing self-orientation and others-orientation involves a high level of self-awareness and adaptability. Leaders can effectively grow themselves and others by being mindful of the need to spend the right amount of time and energy in serving self and others.

Ambition *and* compassion

Abhay, a startup founder, was more ambitious and driven than those around him. While this was necessary for his work, his lack of empathy alienated him from the people around him. If we drive ourselves hard, we expect the same from others, and if we are in a position of power, we will drive others the same way because we can.

On the face of it, ambition and compassion seem to be at two ends of the spectrum. Ambition is all about the drive and the determination to achieve results. Compassion is about connecting with others, caring for them and having a genuine concern for others. Ambition can sometimes come at the cost of the well-being of others. Compassion might sometimes necessitate sacrificing one's drive for results.

Striking the right balance between the two is key for leaders to achieve organization goals without compromising on the well-being of the team. This is easier said than done and requires a great deal of courage, commitment and reflection. Let us examine some of the ways of doing this.

Actively practise self-compassion

Having a personal ambition or an ambition for the organization is something that comes naturally to most leaders. They are focused on creating a vision, setting goals and driving for results. They drive themselves hard, believing it is the only way to succeed. They are hard on others and even more so on themselves.

In her book *Self-Compassion: The Proven Power of Being Kind to Yourself*,[91] Kristin Neff talks about treating oneself with the same care and concern that one would offer to a close friend during times of difficulty. Neff defines self-compassion through three core components.

Self-kindness versus self-judgement: Being kind and gentle towards oneself versus being harsh and overly critical.

Common humanity versus isolation: Recognizing that failures and imperfection are universal human experiences, and not viewing one's problems as unique.

Mindfulness versus over-identification: Being able to observe one's thoughts and feelings from a distance with clarity and without judgement and not get overwhelmed or consumed by negative emotions.

Practising the above will increase self-acceptance, resilience and perseverance in leaders and help them to navigate setbacks with a positive frame of mind. This will lead to lower levels of anxiety and increased well-being.

The same applies while nurturing others as well. Nurturing leaders demonstrate compassion in their dealings with others, thus enabling them to have lower levels of anxiety, increased well-being and ultimately higher productivity.

Be constructive, not critical

Ambitious leaders constantly strive to achieve results, often at the cost of everything else, leading to stress, anxiety and burnout. In their zeal to achieve success, leaders might become their biggest critics and take things personally.

The inner critic is a voice of self-doubt and self-judgement that can diminish one's confidence and hinder effective decision-making. It can make us doubt our own abilities and potentially take us on a downward spiral. It is important for leaders to recognize that the inner critic is often rooted in fear of failure or an inherent desire for perfection.

Once they are able to do this, the next step is to acknowledge the inner critic without letting it dictate actions or erode self-belief. This is easier said than done and requires a high level of self-awareness and willpower. Nurturing leaders then replace the inner critic with constructive feedback.

They reframe the negative messages of the inner critic into constructive and supportive thoughts, which help them learn and move forward. For example, instead of thinking, 'I'm not good enough to do this,' reframe it to, 'I'm learning, and this challenge is an opportunity for me to grow.' This can boost confidence and create a positive mindset. Nurturing leaders are able to channelize the negative energy of the inner critic in a positive and constructive way, leading to personal growth and happiness.

Working with our inner critic makes it easier to be more constructive with others. Compassionate leaders are able to use radical candour more effectively as they challenge directly and care personally.

Focus on efforts, not just outcome

'It's not the destination; it's the journey,' is a quote famously attributed to American philosopher Ralph Waldo Emerson. While focusing on the results and working towards them is important, it is also important to enjoy the journey, savour the experience and learn from it. Efforts are all about the actions, energy and processes that we invest to achieve our goals. Outcomes are the end results of our efforts, often tied to goals or desired achievements.

While our efforts are very much in our control, outcomes are very often not. Leaders would do well to lean into Stephen Covey's concept of the Circle of Concern and the Circle of Influence.[92] The Circle of Concern includes things that individuals are concerned about but have no control over, such as the weather, sports or global politics. The Circle of Influence includes things that individuals can influence but do not have complete control over, such as their relationships, their work environment and their health. The more time we spend in the circle of concern, the more anxious we become; we get into victim mode, and the circle of concern keeps expanding. However, if we spend more time on what is in our control, we feel more confident, the circle of influence keeps expanding, and we get into a growth mode.

Leaders who focus their energies on their efforts and that of their team foster adaptability, learning and growth. This helps them and their teams to try our creative solutions, learn fast and move on. This enhances the overall learning curve of the team and gets them ready to take on new challenges.

Leaders need to recognize that efforts are the foundation for growth, learning and persistence, while outcomes reflect the ultimate purpose of those efforts and are essential for accountability and impact. Great leaders and teams balance both: valuing effort while steering it toward meaningful outcomes. By aligning processes with results, organizations and individuals can create environments that motivate, innovate, and achieve results in a sustainable manner.

Nurturing leaders need to create and maintain the right balance between seemingly conflicting forces in order to be able to effectively nurture themselves and others. They can do this by deciding where in the spectrum they want to be and then mindfully working towards striking the right balance by being fully present to the situation at hand. This will help them effectively navigate the world of the AND.

STRIKING THE RIGHT BALANCE

15
Bringing It All Together

We have so far seen that there are various kinds of challenges that leaders face in today's world, and that these fall under four broad categories: **macro, business, people** and **personal** challenges. These challenges take a toll on leaders, deplete their energy and impact their well-being. Leaders need to regularly nurture themselves to replenish their depleted energies.

We then introduced the concept of **Nurturing Leadership**, measured through the Nurturing Quotient (NQ), on why it is important for leaders to regularly nurture themselves so that they can perform to their potential, and they can then effectively nurture others. We have created a tool that helps one carry out a self-audit to see where they stand in terms of nurturing the self and others.

Nurturing the self is about enhancing their **PMES** (**physical, mental, emotional** and **spiritual**) well-being. **Nurturing others** is about effectively nurturing others through the qualities of **HOPE**—humility, openness, patience and empathy—while following the steps of **preparing** the soil, **planting** the seeds, **providing** water and sunshine and **pulling out** the weeds.

To do this effectively, four key nurturing behaviours are required: **mentoring and coaching, inspiring, listening** and **empowering** (**MILE**). We spoke to over 115 leaders to understand the steps they take to nurture themselves as well as others, and we have shared these best practices of leaders from across organizations, industries and countries. These are simple, practical tips that can easily be adopted by anyone who wants to nurture the self and others.

We saw that the extent of nurturing and the ways of nurturing are a function of many factors, including personality, demographics, values and beliefs and culture. Even after all of this, there are several things that are outside the control of leaders. In this dynamic environment, they need to be able to effectively navigate the ANDs on an everyday basis to be a truly nurturing leader. These ANDs are around discipline *and* flexibility, self-orientation *and* others-orientation, ambition *and* compassion. Knowing where one wants to be on that spectrum and continually managing it is key to successful leadership.

Leaders are at various stages of this journey. When it comes to nurturing ourselves, some of us may be good at nurturing ourselves physically and mentally but low on emotional and spiritual nurturing. Similarly, while nurturing others, some of us could be good at mentoring and empowering but low on listening.

Irrespective of where we are on this journey, it is important for us to continue to take it forward. This involves unlearning and relearning. It also involves the creation of new habits and maybe giving up on some current habits that no longer serve us on our journey. Writing this book has made us aware of how we nurture ourselves and others.

We present a framework below to help aspiring leaders embark on this journey of creating new habits and practices that will enable them to nurture themselves and others more effectively. We call this framework **AISH: Awareness, Intention, Start action** and **Habit creation**. We will examine each of these in some detail. AISH in Hindi means delight and enjoyment, which we believe is the outcome of creating new habits to nurture the self and others.

HABIT CREATION PROCESS (AISH)

Awareness

It all begins with us doing some self-reflection and becoming aware of ourselves. This self-reflection can help us understand our strengths and opportunities, our personalities, as well as our drivers and derailers and so on. This kind of self-reflection requires setting aside some me-time, practising mindfulness and having an open mind. We can glean further insights about ourselves by actively soliciting feedback from others.

There are also several tools that give us a sense of who we are across different dimensions. The Nurturing Quotient-NQ Assessment that we introduced in the book is one such tool that tells us where we are today on the various aspects of nurturing ourselves and nurturing others. You can access the tool by scanning the QR code found on page 36 and 252 in this book. The results of this tool, when combined with other personal insights, can help us identify the areas that we need to work upon to nurture ourselves and others.

For example, leaders who assess themselves using the tool might find that they are relatively low on nurturing themselves spiritually, especially in the dimension of having a purpose. This awareness is important to then help set an intention to do something about it, like creating a personal mission statement. Another leader may find that they are low on the dimension of active listening when it comes to nurturing others, which might lead to learning some techniques for active listening. This level of awareness is the starting point for bringing about a change within.

Intention

Once there is a base level of self-awareness, one then needs to set an intention to do something about it. Setting the right intention is foundational to pretty much anything that we want to achieve—attaining personal growth, furthering our leadership journey or managing relationships. An intention acts as a compass, providing clarity, direction and purpose to actions and decisions.

We have limited time and energy in our hands. Having the right intention helps us make the right choices in terms of what we choose to do with that finite time and energy. These choices are usually aligned to our core values and purpose. Intention gives us clarity and energy. It energizes us to take action. Intention is about 'being' and is a precursor to taking action, which is all about 'doing'.

Some examples of setting intentions are 'I will communicate openly with my partner', 'I intend to empower my team to enable them to grow' or 'I will start exercising to become fit'. The right intention often acts as a bridge between our values and our actions. It ensures that we work with a sense of purpose and authenticity, thereby creating meaningful outcomes.

Intention involves active choice. None of the actions required are dramatically new or extremely difficult. We usually know what we really need to do. The intention is the starting point for a long-lasting commitment.

Start action

While it is important to have a high level of self-awareness and then set the right intention, it is equally important to take the necessary action. How often do we attend an inspirational training programme, come back fully charged to make changes in our life, only for it to fizzle away within a week? We draw up a set of New Year's resolutions around exercising, eating right or reading, which lasts just for a few days or weeks.

So, what gets in the way of us taking action?

It could be inertia, of being in that state where nothing changes. It could be procrastination, the innate desire to postpone things, especially those that are considered 'unpleasant'. It could be overthinking—being in a state of prolonged analysis paralysis. Or it could be setting lofty goals that don't ever lead to any action.

We could have a limiting belief or a fear of change that prevents us from taking a new action. Professor Robert Keegan and Lisa Lahey, in their book *Immunity to Change*, emphasize the importance of working on our mindsets to enable us to change behaviours.[93] We have competing commitments and big assumptions that create a barrier for a new change and keep us doing the same things in the same way even though we may consciously admit that we are ready for change.

Working with a coach—health coach, life coach, relationship coach or an executive coach—can be helpful to identity the deep seated mindsets that prevent us from starting and sustaining action.

Here are some things we can do to sustain action.

- Visualize the long-term gain so that it becomes more attractive than the short-term pain.
- Keep the goals **SMART—specific, measurable, attainable, realistic** and **time-bound**.
- Keep things simple.
- Talk about it to others; apply positive pressure on yourself.
- Put it out in the universe.

You can choose one or more of the above, but the important thing is to get started and keep at it.

Habit formation

Creating good habits involves a process of becoming aware, setting an intention, starting an action and continuing the action over time. Sustained action taken over an extended period of time leads to habit formation. While creating new habits, it is important to aim for consistency over perfection. Once we are able to consistently do something new and create a habit, perfection will follow.

Create the right environment to support habit formation. If you are trying to stop eating junk food, stop stocking it at home. Also focus on becoming that person who embodies that habit. Instead of saying 'I want to exercise', tell yourself 'I value my health and hence would like to exercise regularly'. It then becomes an identity-based habit.

There are several hacks for creating new habits; some of these are listed below.

- Start small, take baby steps and then slowly ramp up—start by running for ten minutes; gradually increase to fifteen minutes, then to twenty and so on.
- Stack a new action that one would like to take against an already existing habit—pick up a book to read as soon as you put down your toothbrush post brushing at night.
- Enrol a buddy to build accountability.
- Track progress over time.
- Celebrate small wins—give yourself a treat upon achieving mini milestones.

Following this framework of **AISH** can help us in our journey of creating and continuing with a set of habits and practices that will help us effectively nurture ourselves and nurture others.

In the years that we wrote this book, 2023–25, we came across several news items about employees committing suicide due to work-related pressures and CEOs suffering heart attacks due to stress. Not only is this scary, but it is also not sustainable for a growing economy.

We believe that everyone needs to find a better way to live and work at every stage of life. You cannot call yourself successful if you have a billion dollars in the bank but have a bad family life and no close friend who has your back. You cannot be successful if you are in the pink of health but your organization has a balance sheet that is all red. You will never be successful at scale if you don't have a circle of people supporting you, cheering you on and lifting you up.

We believe that Nurturing Leadership offers a path for those who want to make an impact at scale AND lead a happy, holistic life filled with joy, purpose and meaning. Enhancing your nurturing quotient (NQ) takes you further on the path towards sustainable growth for everyone.

We are on that journey ourselves, and we hope that this book will benefit others on their journey as well.

Acknowledgements

The Nurturing Quotient began with the seed of an idea that turned into a book with the support of literally hundreds of people.

We, Rajesh and Nirupama, are grateful to our parents for providing the nurturing required during our growing-up years, which has enabled us to nurture this book to life. We hope to continue to have your blessings.

Our daughter Kaavya has allowed us to experience the joys of parenting, which is the first and a lifelong experiment in nurturing. We hope to do better as we both grow!

Thank you to Prema Govindan, our agent and friend, for finding us a home for the manuscript with Penguin Random House India, which was our first choice.

The team at Penguin Random House India—Radhika Marwah, Manish Kumar, Manali Das and Aninda Das—have been very enthusiastic and supportive of *The Nurturing Quotient* and have nurtured the manuscript to reach its potential as a book. Thanks to Sparsh Raj Singh for the cover design.

Thank you to our illustrator, Vaishnav S., for bringing the concept to life with the illustrations.

Amaara Singh, a bright young intern, has supported us through the editing process of the book.

Acknowledgements

Thank you to the team from Green Thumbs, led by Neha and Ankur Manchanda, who have helped us create the Nurturing Quotient (NQ) assessment tool.

The richness of this book comes from the conversations we've had with several leaders who candidly and generously shared their experiences of how they nurture themselves and others. We initially thought we would speak to twenty-five to thirty CEOs to get their inputs, but we eventually ended up conducting our primary research with 118 leaders.

This would not have been possible without the introductions and connections from some generous people. Thank you, Anshika Dhawan, Ashish Parikh, Atri Sengupta, Deepika Bahn, Deepak Jayaraman, Jessie Zhang, Kaushika Madhavan, Manish Sinha, Mannu Bhatia, Nikhil Dey, Nupur Bhargava, Pavan Bhatia, Payal Jindal Khanna, R. Mahalakshmi, Reema Malhotra, Sakshi Handa, Sathya Sriram, Shibani Sethi, Siddharth Agarwal, Toral Patel, Varsha Kanal and Vishal Malik.

We are grateful to Ira Trivedi and Kavita Devgan for their expert inputs on well-being.

Our chapter on mentoring and coaching would not have been complete without the contributions from those who have recognized the value of their mentors and shared their experience with us—Aparna M. Vishwasrao, Manshul Nagpal, Mayank Pandey, Nupur Goenka, Rachna Kanwar, Rahul Choudhary, Vineet Sharma and Vipul Sabharwal.

We truly appreciate the endorsements for the book from the eminent leaders who live this concept and believe in the cause.

We would like to thank Nitin Paranjpe for the foreword, which truly captures the essence of the concept and its relevance in today's world. Thank you so much for bringing this alive in such an evocative manner.

Acknowledgements

Finally, this book would not have been possible without the enriching and insightful conversations with the following leaders from around the world. Each interview sparked new ideas and gave us rich content to work with as we wrote this book.

Thank you, thank you, thank you.

List of leaders and organizations

Lt General A.K. Bhatt (retd)	Indian Space Association
Vice Admiral A.K. Chawla (retd)	Indian Navy
Achal Agarwal	ex-Kimberly Clark
Aditya Ghosh	Akasa Air
Aditya Sehgal	ex-Reckitt
Alok Mittal	Indifi Technologies Pvt. Ltd
Alpana Titus	Reckitt
Amit Jain	Sanofi CHC and Collective Newsroom
Amit Syngle	Asian Paints
Amrita Randhawa	Publicis Groupe Asia Pacific
Apurva Purohit	Aazol
Anand Kripalu	EPL
Anant Goel	Milkbasket
V. Anantha Nageswaran	chief economic adviser (GOI)
Anil Arjun	Storiculture
Anupriya Acharya	Publicis Groupe, South Asia
Anuradha Acharya	MapmyGenome
Anusha Shetty	Grey India
Arnab Banerjee	CEAT Limited
Arundhati Bhattacharya	Salesforce
Ashish Dhawan	The Convergence Foundation

Ayushi Gudwani	FS Life
B. Govinda Rajan	Royal Enfield
Bharat Puri	Pidilite Industries
Binu Jacob	Nestlé India
Clive Kornitzer	OSB Group PLC
Debjani Ghosh	ex-NASSCOM
Deep Kalra	MakeMyTrip
Deepak Iyer	Mondelēz
Deepak Jayaraman	ex-McKinsey & Company
Narasimhan Eswar	Whirlpool
Gabriel Fernández	Mars Wrigley
Geetika Mehta	Nivea
Govind Iyer	Infosys
Greet Boonen	RainPharma
Harish Devarajan	ex-Unilever
Harit Nagpal	Tata Play
Harsh Mariwala	Marico
Hemant Malik	ITC Foods
Hephzibah Pathak	Ogilvy
Hina Nagarajan	Diageo
Hitesh Oberoi	Info Edge
Jagrut Kotecha	PepsiCo
Kalpesh Parmar	Mars Wrigley
Kaushik Mukherjee	SUGAR Cosmetics
Kedar Lele	Castrol
Kirthiga Reddy	Verix and ex-Meta India
Madhav Kalyan	JP Morgan
Magdalena Nowicka Mook	International Coaching Federation
Mahesh Madhavan	Bacardi
Malika Datt Sadaani	The Moms Co.
Mamta Saikia	Bharti Foundation

Mansi Tripathy	Shell
Manu Anand	ex-Mondelēz AMEA and ex-PepsiCo India
Meenakshi Nevatia	Pfizer
Melda Yasar Cebe	ex-Kraft Heinz
Mike Spanos	Bloomin' Brands
Mohit Anand	Kellanova
Mohit Sadaani	The Moms Co.
N.P. Singh	ex-Sony Pictures
Narmeen Khan	Mondelēz
Naveen Munjal	Hero Electric Vehicles
Navneet Saluja	Haleon
Neil George	Abbott Nutrition
Neetu Kashiramka	VIP Industries
Nisaba Godrej	Godrej Group
Nitish Kapoor	Reckitt
Pankaj Saran	ex-deputy NSA
Pankajam Sridevi	ex-Commonwealth Bank
Dr Parag Rindani	Wockhardt Hospitals
Pavan Bhatia	ex-PepsiCo
Prakash Iyer	ex-Kimberly Clark
Pramath Sinha	Ashoka University
Pranab Barua	ex-Aditya Birla Group
Puneet Chandok	Microsoft
Puneet Davar	Tropilite
Radhika Gupta	Edelweiss Mutual Fund
Radhika Piramal	VIP Industries
Raghu Krishnan	Kenvue
Rahul Shankar	Quest Retail
Rajeev Dubey	ex-Mahindra & Mahindra
Rajesh Jejurikar	Mahindra & Mahindra
Rajiv Rajgopal	AkzoNobel
Rakesh Sharma	Bajaj Auto

Ram Raghavan	Colgate-Palmolive
Ramesh Mangaleswaran	McKinsey & Company
Ratna Viswanathan	Reach to Teach
Ritesh Gauba	pladis Global
C.V.L. Srinivas	WPP Group
Sameer Suneja	Perfetti Van Melle
Sameer Wadhawan	ex-Samsung
Sandeep Kataria	Bata
Sandeep Sangwan	Castrol
Santosh Iyer	Mercedes-Benz
Sanjiv Mehta	ex-Unilever and L Catterton India
Sathya Sriram	ex-Apollo Preventive Care
Shiv Shivakumar	Advent International
Sivakumar Sundaram	Bennett and Coleman
Sridhar Balakrishnan	Duroflex
Sucheta Govil	Covestro
Sudhir Sitapati	Godrej Consumer Products Ltd
Sunil D'Souza	Tata Consumer Products
Suparna Mitra	Titan Watches
Suresh Narayanan	Nestlé India
Susanne Arfelt Rajamand	ex-Royal Greenland
Tarun Arora	Zydus Wellness
Toshan Tamhane	UPL
Uday Shankar Sinha	Heineken
Uttam Digga	Porter
Varun Berry	Britannia
Vignesh Nandakumar	Enfinity Global
Vijay Subramaniam	Bacardi
Vikas Chawla	Compass Group India
Vikas Srivastava	ex-Johnson & Johnson Consumer (India)

Vineet Nayar	ex-HCL Technologies
Vineeta Singh	SUGAR Cosmetics
Vinita Bali	ex-Britannia Industries
Vivek Gambhir	Lightspeed
Yamini Bhat	Vymo

Notes

1. Nirupama Subramanian, *Powerful: The Indian Woman's Guide to Unlocking Her Full Potential* (HarperCollins, 2021).
2. Nicolai Chen Nielsen, Gemma D'Auria and Sasha Zolley, 'Tuning in, Turning Outward: Cultivating Compassionate Leadership in a Crisis', McKinsey & Company, 1 May 2020, https://www.mckinsey.com/capabilities/people-and-organizational-performance/our-insights/tuning-in-turning-outward-cultivating-compassionate-leadership-in-a-crisis.
3. 'BANI—Living in the Age of Chaos', 26 April 2022, https://ageofbani.com/.
4. Ronald A. Heifetz and Marty Linsky, *Adaptive Leadership: The Heifetz Collection (3 Items)* (Harvard Business Review Press, 2014).
5. 'Insights', KPMG, n.d., https://kpmg.com/xx/en/our-insights.html.
6. 'The Deloitte Global Millennial Survey 2019', Deloitte, 2019, https://www2.deloitte.com/content/dam/Deloitte/global/Documents/About-Deloitte/deloitte-2019-millennial-survey.pdf.
7. James Scouller, *The Three Levels of Leadership 2nd Edition: How to Develop Your Leadership Presence, Knowhow and Skill* (Management Books 2000, 2016).
8. Indra Nooyi, *My Life in Full: Work, Family and Our Future* (Hachette UK, 2021).
9. Megan Cerullo, 'Nearly 3 Million U.S. Women Have Dropped Out of the Labor Force in the Past Year', CBS

News, 5 February 2021, https://www.cbsnews.com/news/covid-crisis-3-million-women-labor-force/.

10 Jennifer Petriglieri, *Couples That Work: How To Thrive in Love and at Work* (Penguin UK, 2019).

11 W. Timothy Gallwey, *The Inner Game of Work: Focus, Learning, Pleasure, and Mobility in the Workplace* (National Geographic Books, 2001).

12 'How Unilever Develops Leaders to Be a Force for Good—Forbes', n.d., https://www.potentialproject.com/insights/how-unilever-develops-leaders-to-be-a-force-for-good.

13 '"You Can Lead Just Like Me": New Zealand's Jacinda Ardern Delivers Farewell Speech', https://www.youtube.com/watch?v=Qb2H85Nq7WU (accessed 20 April 2025).

14 'CEO Tenure Rates', The Harvard Law School Forum on Corporate Governance, 4 August 2023, https://corpgov.law.harvard.edu/2023/08/04/ceo-tenure-rates-2/ .

15 'Drop Dead: Stress is the silent killer of top-performing CEOs; Here's how to deal with it', CEO Coaching International, https://ceocoachinginternational.com/managing-stress/.

16 Mark Borgschulte et al., 'CEO Stress, Aging, and Death', 1 March 2021, https://doi.org/10.3386/w28550 .

17 'Egon Zehnder Asked Over 400 of the World's Top CEOs What They Found Harder Than Expected When They Took the Top Job', Egon Zehnder, 8 August 2023, https://www.egonzehnder.com/press-release/egon-zehnder-asked-over-400-of-the-worlds-top-ceos-what-they-found-harder-than-expected-when-they-took-the-top-job .

18 C. Maslach, W.B. Schaufeli, M.P. Leiter, 'Job Burnout', https://pubmed.ncbi.nlm.nih.gov/11148311/

19 Jason Ma, 'CEOs have never headed for the exits as much as they are this year—here's why so many are leaving', *Fortune*, 22 December 2024, https://fortune.com/2024/12/22/ceo-exits-record-high-us-corporate-leadership-changes-top-reasons/.

20 Jen Fisher and Paul H. Silverglate, 'The C-suite's Role in Well-being', Deloitte Insights, 22 June 2022, https://www2.

deloitte.com/us/en/insights/topics/leadership/employee-wellness-in-the-corporate-workplace.html .
21 https://web-assets.bcg.com/img-src/The_Global_Leadership_and_Talent_Index_Mar_2015_tcm9-74599.pdf
22 Sapien Labs Centre for the Human Brain and Mind at Krea University et al., 'Mental State of India: The Internet-enabled Youth', 2023, https://sapienlabs.org/wp-content/uploads/2023/11/Mental-State-of-India-Report-October-2023.pdf .
23 'What Is Purpose?' Greater Good Magazine, https://greatergood.berkeley.edu/topic/purpose/definition.
24 Peter Limbach and Florian Sonnenburg, 'Does CEO Fitness Matter?', Cologne: Centre for Financial Research working paper, 2015, https://www.econstor.eu/bitstream/10419/123715/1/841379122.pdf .
25 Ibid.
26 Peter Attia MD, *Outlive: The Science and Art of Longevity* (Harmony, 2023).
27 'Quitting smoking cuts your risk of developing type 2 diabetes by 30–40%', WHO, 14 November 2023, https://www.who.int/news/item/14-11-2023-quitting-smoking-cuts-your-risk-of-developing-type-2-diabetes-by-30-40 .
28 Peter Attia MD, *Outlive: The Science and Art of Longevity* (Harmony, 2023).
29 Tom Huddleston Jr, 'Melinda French Gates Says CEOs Who Cut Sleep to Maximize Productivity Are "So Dumb": "Some of Us Didn't Want to Be Around Them"', CNBC, 19 September 2024, https://www.cnbc.com/2024/09/19/melinda-french-gates-sleeping-only-a-few-hours-a-night-is-so-dumb.html .
30 'About Sleep', Sleep, 15 May 2024, https://www.cdc.gov/sleep/about/index.html .
31 James Clear, *Atomic Habits: An Easy & Proven Way to Build Good Habits & Break Bad Ones* (Penguin, 2018).
32 Tony Schwartz and Catherine McCarthy, 'Manage Your Energy, Not Your Time', *Harvard Business Review*, October

2007, https://hbr.org/2007/10/manage-your-energy-not-your-time (accessed 20 April 2025).

33 Ankita Sengupta, 'Bill Gates Reveals How He Turned Idle Time into Deep Thinking: "It Was Also Crucial to My Success"', Money Control, 15 December 2024, https://www.moneycontrol.com/news/trends/bill-gates-reveals-how-he-turned-idle-time-into-deep-thinking-it-was-also-crucial-to-my-success-12890172.html (accessed 20 April 2025).

34 Jeremy Sutton, Ph.D. 'Mihály Csíkszentmihályi: The Father of Flow', 31 March 2025, https://positivepsychology.com/mihaly-csikszentmihalyi-father-of-flow/ (accessed 20 April 2025).

35 'The Brain and Neuroplasticity', https://www.hubermanlab.com/topics/brain-and-neuroplasticity.

36 'What Is Emotional Intelligence, Daniel Goleman', Last Eight Percent, 10 December 2024, https://www.ihhp.com/meaning-of-emotional-intelligence/ .

37 Martin E.P. Seligman, *Learned Optimism: How to Change Your Mind and Your Life* (Vintage, 2011).

38 'How Nature Can Make You Kinder, Happier, and More Creative', Greater Good, n.d., https://greatergood.berkeley.edu/article/item/how_nature_makes_you_kinder_happier_more_creative .

39 Seth Stevenson, 'State of Workplace Empathy', Businessolver, 30 September 2024, https://www.businessolver.com/workplace-empathy/ .

40 André Lacroix, *Leadership with Soul: Putting People at the Heart of Your Growth Strategy* (World Scientific Books, 2022).

41 Spiritual Leadership Model, https://iispiritualleadership.com/spiritual-leadership-theory/.

42 Hitendra Wadhwa, *Inner Mastery, Outer Impact: How Your Five Core Energies Hold the Key to Success* (New York: Hachette Book Group, 2022), p. 25.

43 Hitendra Wadhwa, 'Leading in the Flow of Work', *Harvard Business Review*, 14 December 2023, https://hbr.org/2024/01/leading-in-the-flow-of-work .

44 Manny Pham, 'Unilever's CEO on the "New Mode of Leadership"', *Marketing Week*, 2 December 2021, https://www.marketingweek.com/unilever-leadership/ .

45 'Doing Good and Feeling Good: Relationships Between Altruism and Well-being for Altruists, Beneficiaries, and Observers', The World Happiness Report, n.d., https://worldhappiness.report/ed/2023/doing-good-and-feeling-good-relationships-between-altruism-and-well-being-for-altruists-beneficiaries-and-observers/ .

46 Tasha Eurich, *Insight: Why We're Not as Self-Aware as We Think, and How Seeing Ourselves Clearly Helps Us Succeed at Work and in Life* (Crown Business, 2017).

47 Deepak Jayaraman, *Play to Potential: Lead a Full Life, Become the Best You* (Penguin Business, 2024).

48 L. Reave, 'Spiritual values and practices related to leadership effectiveness', *The Leadership Quarterly*, 16(5) (2005), 655–687. https://doi.org/10.1016/j.leaqua.2005.07.003 .

49 Carol S. Dweck, *Mindset: The New Psychology of Success* (National Geographic Books, 2007).

50 Peter A. Heslin and Don Vandewalle, 'Managers' Implicit Assumptions About Personnel', SMU Scholar, n.d., https://scholar.smu.edu/business_management_organizations_research/2/ .

51 https://www.gallup.com/394373/indicator-employee-engagement.aspx

52 Ruchira Chaudhary, *Coaching: The Secret Code to Uncommon Leadership* (Penguin Random House India, 2021).

53 Barry Bozeman, Mary K. Feeney and University of Georgia, Athens, 'Toward a Useful Theory of Mentoring: A Conceptual Analysis and Critique', *Administration & Society* 39 (2007): 719–39, https://www.andrews.edu/ceis/leadership_school/documents/toward_a_useful_theo.pdf .

54 Michael Gill and Thomas Roulet, 'Stressed at Work? Mentoring a Colleague Could Help', 1 March 2019, https://hbr.org/2019/03/stressed-at-work-mentoring-a-colleague-could-help

55 Jim Clifton and Gallup, 'State of the American Manager: Analytics and Advice for Leaders', Gallup, 2015, https://d46w5x9vt7qfg.cloudfront.net/businessreport/2015/04/StateOfAmericanManager_032715_mhLowRes.pdf .

56 Kevin Roberts, *Lovemarks: The Future Beyond Brands* (Simon and Schuster, 2005).

57 Nirupama Subramanian, *Powerful: The Indian Woman's Guide to Unlocking Her Full Potential* (HarperCollins India, 2021).

58 Historic Speeches, https://www.jfklibrary.org/learn/about-jfk/historic-speeches/address-at-rice-university-on-the-nations-space-effort (accessed 20 April 2025).

59 J. Sterling Livingston, 'Pygmalion in Management', *Harvard Business Review*, January 2023, https://hbr.org/2003/01/pygmalion-in-management (accessed 20 April 2025).

60 Sylvia Melena, *Supportive Accountability: How to Inspire People and Improve Performance* (Melena Consulting Group, 2018).

61 Daniel H. Pink, *Drive: The Surprising Truth About What Motivates Us* (Riverhead Books, 2009).

62 'President Obama Reunites with Woman Behind 2008's "Hottest" Campaign Catchphrase', https://www.obama.org/stories/edith-childs/ (accessed 20 April 2025).

63 Jay A. Conger and Rabindra N. Kanungo, 'Charismatic leadership in organizations: perceived behavioral attributes and their measurement', *Journal of Organizational Behavior*, 15(5) (1994), 439–452. https://www.jstor.org/stable/2488215 .

64 R.E. Boyatzis, M.L. Smith and N. Blaize, 'Developing sustainable leaders through coaching and compassion', *Academy of Management Learning and Education*, 2006, https://doi.org/10.5465/amle.2006.20388381 .

65 *Impact of empathetic leadership on organizational Culture* (Goleman, 2000) https://www.google.com/search?q=Impact+of+Empathetic+

Leadership+on+Organizational+Culture+ (Goleman%2C+2000&oq=Impact+of+Empathetic+ Leadership+on+Organizational+Culture+(Goleman %2C+2000&gslcrp=EgZjaHJvbWUyBggAEEUYOdI BBzMwN2owajeoAgCwAgA&sourceid=chrome&ie= UTF-8

66 Barbara L. Fredrickson, 'The Role of Positive Emotions in Positive Psychology: The Broaden-and-Build Theory of Positive Emotions', *American Psychologist* 56, no. 3 (2001): 218, https://peplab.web.unc.edu/wp-content/ uploads/sites/18901/2018/11/fredricksonampsyc2001.pdf .

67 Prof. Richard Peterson, 'Understanding the Ladder of Inference: Navigating Cognitive Pitfalls', USC Gould School of Law, 28 November 2023, https://gould.usc.edu/news/understanding-the- ladder-of-inference-navigating-cognitive-pitfalls/ (accessed 20 April 2025).

68 Stephen R. Covey, *The Seven Habits of Highly Effective People: Restoring the Character Ethic* (1997).

69 Sylvia Ann Hewitt, 'The New Rules of Executive Presence', *Harvard Business Review*, January–February 2024, https:// hbr.org/2024/01/the-new-rules-of-executive-presence .

70 Jim Collins, *Good to Great: Why Some Companies Make the Leap . . . and Others Don't* (HarperBusiness, 2001).

71 Nancy Kline, *Time to Think: Listening to Ignite the Human Mind*. Cassell, 2002.

72 'The Top 50 Listening Leaders', Sideways, 1 February 2023, https://ideas.sideways6.com/article/the-top-50- listening-leaders .

73 'Microsoft CEO Satya Nadella: How I Work, *Wall Street Journal*, 30 September 2015, https://www.wsj.com/video/ microsoft-ceo-satya-nadella-how-i-work/4F6C3478-0AB5- 4A77-B175-E36590EEAC07.

74 Jack Zenger and Joe Folkman, 'What Great Listeners Actually Do', 2019, https://zengerfolkman.com/wp-

content/uploads/2019/08/What-Great-Listeners-Actually-Do_WP-2019.pdf (accessed 20 April 2025).
75 'The David Rubenstein Show: Satya Nadella', *Bloomberg*, 25 October 2017, https://www.bloomberg.com/news/videos/2017-10-25/the-david-rubenstein-show-satya-nadella-video.
76 'The Power of Empathy in Times of Crisis and Beyond', Catalyst, n.d., https://www.catalyst.org/insights/2021/empathy-work-strategy-crisis .
77 'Why Mars boss Poul Weihrauch wants to help others on climate goals', TIME, 10 December 2023, https://time.com/6344262/mars-ceo-poul-weihrauch-interview/.
78 Daniel Goleman, *Focus: The Hidden Driver of Excellence* (HarperCollins, 2013).
79 '2022 Special Report: Trust in the Workplace', Edelman, n.d., https://www.edelman.com/trust/2022-trust-barometer/special-report-trust-workplace#:~:text=78%%20of%20employees%20trust%20their%20employer.%2069%,manager%2C%20head%20of%20HR%20and%20their%20CEO .
80 'Building Trust in Business and Leadership', Deloitte, 27 May 2024, https://www.deloitte.com/global/en/issues/trust.html .
81 *Understand Team Effectiveness.* Google re:Work, Google, https://rework.withgoogle.com/guides/understanding-team-effectiveness.
82 Amy C. Edmondson, 'The Fearless Organization: Creating Psychological Safety in the Workplace for Learning, Innovation and Growth', https://amycedmondson.com/psychological-safety/ (accessed 20 April 2025).
83 'What Is Psychological Safety?', McKinsey & Company, 17 July 2023, https://www.mckinsey.com/featured-insights/mckinsey-explainers/what-is-psychological-safety .

84 Ken Blanchard, 'Feedback Is the Breakfast of Champions', 17 August 2009, https://www.kenblanchardbooks.com/feedback-is-the-breakfast-of-champions/ (accessed 20 April 2025)
85 Kim Scott, *Radical Candor: Be a Kick-Ass Boss Without Losing Your Humanity* (St. Martin's Press, 2017).
86 History of DiSC®: Decades of research and real-world applications, Disc Profile, https://www.discprofile.com/what-is-disc/history-of-disc (accessed 20 April 2025).
87 James Clear, *Atomic Habits* (Random House, 2018).
88 Kimberly Schaufenbuel, 'Why Google, Target, and General Mills Are Investing in Mindfulness', *Harvard Business Review*, 30 August 2021, https://hbr.org/2015/12/why-google-target-and-general-mills-are-investing-in-mindfulness .
89 Reed Hastings and Erin Meyer, *No Rules Rules: Netflix and the Culture of Reinvention* (Penguin, 2020).
90 Megan Sauer, 'Netflix co-founder says this weekly ritual keeps him successful: I've done it "for over 30 years",' make it, 13 June 2024, https://www.cnbc.com/2024/06/13/netflix-co-founder-this-weekly-ritual-has-helped-me-succeed-for-30-years.html#:~:text=Randolph%20credited%20that%20balance%20largely,evening%20with%20my%20best%20friend.%22 (accessed 20 April 2025).
91 Kristin Neff, *Self-Compassion: The Proven Power of Being Kind to Yourself* (HarperCollins, 2011).
92 Anna Katharina Schaffner, 'Understanding the Circles of Control, Influence & Concern', 1 June 2023, https://positivepsychology.com/circles-of-influence/ (accessed on 20 April 2025).
93 Robert Kegan and Lisa Laskow Lahey, *Immunity to Change: How to Overcome It and Unlock the Potential in Yourself and Your Organization* (Harvard Business Review Press, 2009).

You can scan the QR code above to take The Nurturing Quotient Assessment to find out your NQ. The report will give you your scores on Nurturing Self and Nurturing Others along with specific areas for further development.